ONE FINE HOUR

ONE FINE HOUR

by *Frederick Keller Stamm*

Harper & Brothers, Publishers, New York

Library of Congress catalog card number: 53–10978

To

All the younger ministers who stood with me as assistants over the years. May their spirits ever be the candles of the Lord

Contents

Acknowledgments

My thanks are due to those from whose writings I have been privileged to quote. Also to Miss Beatrice M. Sims for typing the manuscript.

F. K. S.

ONE FINE HOUR

I

A Venture upon God into the Unknown

THERE was nothing traditional about Jesus of Nazareth. The greatest fact about him was the consciousness of an inner creativeness that would not allow him to turn his activity into traditional channels. He refused to be the "Great Baker, the Great Conqueror, and the Great Miracle Worker. He left behind the three ideals of his time, and of ours: the materialism of the Sadducees, the power policy of the Romans, and the spiritual totalitarianism of the Pharisees." [1] If the Kingdom of Heaven which was the burden of his life and his teaching, and for which the Church prays in the Lord's Prayer, should ever become a reality, neither he nor his followers could walk in the beaten track. It had to be based on a new relationship with God whom he called "Father." God's will had to be supreme, and what inner creativeness belonged to Jesus had first to belong to his Father. There was no guarantee that anything he set out to do could be accomplished if he misused his power for anything aside from his Father's will.

It ought to be clear to every preacher, to every teacher of youth, and to every leader of the *Ecclesia,* that Jesus' consciousness of God was not the result of an idea or theory about God. He never defined God, and he never argued about God. If ever anyone had asked him to give a conclusive demonstration as to the existence of God, he would have looked at the questioner in wonder and bewilderment. What he did was to assume God and to live on the basis of God. This is not to say this basis was a vague unanalyzable feeling, but an intuition with rational content similar in all respects to our experience in the love of the most intimate relationship with any friend with whom we ever lived.

Nor was Jesus' rapport with the mind and spirit of his Father something that came and went, like the intermittent contact of a man with his friend. When one reads the story of his life, one feels that with the exception of that dread moment on the Cross, there never was a time when he stood in any other relationship with God than that of feeling the divine power coursing through his mind, body and spirit. It was a profound experience which he gained in his home in Nazareth, out under the stars, as he climbed the hills, and walked amidst the flowers of the field. But more than that, it

2

came from the knowledge that for long centuries his race had been in search of God, had hoped for a new social order where "the earth shall be full of the knowledge of the Lord, as the waters cover the sea." [2] Somewhere there had to be a Man whose spirit would be God-possessed, and who would be a witness of what God could do, not only for a single individual, but for the world.

When Jesus prayed, "I thank thee, O Father, Lord of heaven and earth, that thou didst hide these things from the wise and understanding, and didst reveal them unto babes: yea, Father, for so it is well-pleasing in thy sight," [3] we hear the pleading voice of a child of God, a seeker, a hungry soul, a man poor in spirit, willing to endure failure, defeat and suffering, if only he can be sure that he is doing the will of God. All the emotion and all the tense, deep feeling of a little child crying on his mother's knee, is wrapped up in that personal petition. The other passage, "All things are delivered unto me of my Father: and no man knoweth the Son, but the Father; neither knoweth any man the Father, save the Son, and he to whomsoever the Son will reveal him," [4] strikes the honest seeker after the mind of Jesus, not as the words of Jesus, but "as an abstract Christological statement that betrays nothing of the warmth which we sense at once in the first. . . . It is a deposit of early Christian conviction and thought." [5]

The truth, however, of Jesus' confidence and trust in God as an abiding experience lies in both the prayer of Jesus and the filial relationship which the early Church believed existed between God and Jesus. Who can deny that Jesus saw the surgent will of God beating up through life and time, and that he read the secrets of the Eternal Heart and then laid himself in perfect obedience beneath it all? Nowhere else do we find a life perfectly woven without seam throughout, from that crisis hour at the age of twelve when the direction of his life was not a thing arbitrarily imposed upon him from above, but which welled up from within in favor of morality and freedom. It was his task to lead a God-estranged world back to God by the way which was opened to him by an unbroken communion with his Father.

When one follows Jesus in his prayers, sits with him at the banquet table, walks with him as he strolls through the fields, sees the humor that plays about his mouth and twinkles in his eyes, or hears him speak words of comfort to the sad and sorrowing, and words of denunciation against the unjust and cruel, there is always the awesome breath of loneliness about him, loneliness in the sense of having an experience which the rest of the world about him does not have. He never removed himself from men. He loved them. But he was always being misunderstood and betrayed even by love.

The populace, not even the disciples, the friends in the Bethany home, or his mother and brethren, stood on the heights of his dreams or the mountain of his vision. Only God could know.

When he saw God's designs, no one stood beside him. His one compensation was the fact that he shared the companionship of God. He seemed to be alone, but he was not alone, for the Father was with him. His consciousness of God's presence was never that of a self withdrawn from the outer world after the manner of medieval monasticism, or of our modern priestly and theological provincialism which substitutes ecclesiastical dogma for the warmth and breadth of the spirit of Jesus. It was a holy fellowship, a mutual in-dwelling of Father and Son. Men have called him God, but he is more human than we—more generous, brave, gentle, forgiving, and more merciful—and yet more divine than any divinity of which man has dreamed. He never asked to be worshiped, only to be followed. When we look about and ask, is there anything real? we reach out our hand and touch him, the one reality our souls can trust.

How did Jesus come by this God-consciousness? What went on in his soul toward its accomplishment? Jesus is always breaking out for me, and becoming something other than the theologians have made him. I could not in my younger days, and I cannot now, place

5

him intellectually, but it is just as impossible to do without him practically. I have read books on theology from Augustine to our day, and followed the winding paths of their speculations. I know the creeds and have read the writings of deists, pantheists, seers, saints, mystics, prophets, and the teachers of old theology and the new— Barthians and liberals of many tints of thought. They teach me many things, but none of them tell me nor do they all put together, what Jesus is to me. And I cannot tell it all in this book, because as life deepens, he means more and more, as inescapable as he is unfathomable.

I have tried to say here what I have long wanted to say, but never seemed to have time to say it. Perhaps I had no right to say it before, for even now I can give only a broken fragment of a life and mind that stood where God stood. He is the unveiling of God such as no philosophy has ever attained, and as much as I have set down about him satisfies my intellect and wins my heart. The force I see moving through history, and the figure I see walking in Palestine, are one and the same. When I question the creeds, they leave me cold. When I question him, a silence falls on me, and I feel he is questioning me. When I walk with him in the days of his flesh he walks with me in this strange age and tries to communicate to my dull mind the solution of its perplexing problems.

A Venture upon God into the Unknown

I do not know all the answers. I know only that Jesus released a power in the world that enables me to do the thing I know I ought to do. When I see him in the midst of his environment I catch a vague hint of the turbulence, the misery, the woe and the anguish of our day. I do not know the shape of things to come, or just how evil will be turned to good, but when I see him, I am constrained to believe that there is a time coming when the soul of man shall be free, and humanity shall live together in one Beloved Community. Taught by Jesus, I see God everywhere, in everything, loving all and forgetting none, and fulfilling his purpose of good will in the world. This I have believed from the day I entered the ministry, and this I hope will continue to grow and thrive in my soul until death hangs his sickle at my garden gate. To me Jesus is not a theory, but a living Reality. The challenge, now as ever, is not to a creed but a Life, and what that challenge will mean in the days ahead will depend on how much faith we have in the Man who was crucified because he loved God and man.

To think, to speak, to write an any other terms than those of the theologian lays one open to criticism, for the obvious reason that theology builds its case on substance or nature and establishes that position by some process of metaphysical reasoning. It is not the purpose here to engage in a theological debate, nor to make any

7

further contribution to the divisions which have torn Christendom asunder and obscured the pure spirit of Jesus. The Church will doubtless go on for a long time to come putting Jesus in a certain category as the result of speculative minds, and rejecting all other ideas as essentially irreligious.

But there are questions no one can escape: Did Jesus possess any other form of religious consciousness than that which identifies him as one in substance and nature with God? Were his home instruction, his listening to his teachers, his study of the prophets, his discipline as a carpenter, his attendance at the worship in the synagogue, and his stealing away into the silences for communion with his Father, only make-believe? Did the first definite and decisive invasion of his soul by the Spirit of God come no earlier than the baptism at the Jordan? Was his case unique in the sense that a certain transcendent world of spirit descended upon a soul that was sinless? Does it make the religious value of his life greater to base the coming of God into time through a birth in which natural law was suspended? Do we make faith more real when we substitute mystery for reason? To be sure, somewhere out of the hidden depths of history he came, with all the goodness of all the ages converging in one single personality to lead and lift us to the heights of true greatness. Here at last was the instrument perfectly attuned to the long patience of God.

And God was waiting for someone to look up into his face and utter the mystic name, "Father," and to which God could answer, "My Son." It was deep, not only calling unto deep, but listening and answering back. It is not in his birth, but in this human and psychological situation that we find the key to his sinlessness.

The one great fact in the thought processes of Israel, and which was won at great cost, was the consciousness of the unity of God. Although this Nazareth boy was born and raised in an environment of a hundred political, religious and social ideas, the one thing to which he had to attune his soul was the spiritual consciousness of his race in accordance with natural psychical law. Whatever spiritual quality a man inherits, it can begin to operate only after birth, and the individual self-consciousness of what is good and right and true is evoked within and by the surrounding social consciousness of the home where father-love and mother-love are supreme.

It was so with Jesus. The consciousness of the unity of God was present in every Jewish home and laid its hand upon every member of the household. It was in this atmosphere that Jesus was born and reared, and later lived and worked. He was a Hebrew of the Hebrews and a Palestinian of the Palestinians, and though refusing to conform to many of the current modes of thought and conduct, this God-environment which elevated the national consciousness to a spiritual dimension was the inescapable and the immediate stimulus of his own course of action.

It was the privilege and the duty of every Jewish parent to teach the young, expanding child-mind, in its first attempt at speech, to repeat the great Shema. It was the first word of religion that the little child took upon his lips. It was fastened in the mezuzah [6] at the door post of his home. It was stitched into the corners of his little robe, and the tassels on the robes of adults called it constantly to mind. It was spoken at meal hour, and was included in the morning and evening prayer. Every Jew lisped it when he awoke in the early morning hour, and before the lights were lit in the evening he intoned it in the presence of the assembled family. It was Israel's creed, and every synagogue worship was begun: "Hear, O Israel: the Lord our God is one Lord." [7]

The religious imperative which followed when Jesus quoted this passage, "Thou shalt love the Lord thy God and thy neighbor as thyself; on these two commandments hang all the law and prophets," became the imperative of his teaching. Josephus says that a Jew will more readily recall his sacred laws than he will his own name because he learned them with the very dawn of his consciousness.[8] One may well say that this national Jewish tradition could become only a stubborn prejudice, as it did in the minds of many Jewish inhabitants.

But not so with Jesus: he elevated it with a new sense of dignity, purity and beauty.

It is a great asset to have the soul lifted so early to the height of a profound spiritual fact. But that is only the beginning. Its completion comes when the precocious soul goes through its own desert experience and when it stands before some burning bush of imagination and insight and hears the voice of the great "I Am." [9]

He learned it at his mother's knee, not in any mechanical fashion such as repeating words formed upon his mother's lips. He imbibed her emotional sources, and every fiber of his soul was awake with wonder and awe. As James Martineau says in one of his sermons, "When a mother calls her children to her knees to speak to them of God, she is herself the greatest object of their affection. It is by her power over them that God becomes venerable, by the purity of her eye that he becomes holy, by the silence of her heart that he becomes awful, but the tenderness of her heart that he becomes dear."

The Nazareth family belonged to the Hasidim, the pious folk, and in the breast of every Jewish family there was the consciousness of being the called and chosen of God. Hearts throbbed with expectation, and we may be sure that Mary's most anxious care was to guard the growing mind of the child from any shadow of doubt and sin that may have crossed her own soul. As a wise mother she would do nothing to perplex the heart of her child.

In a novel familiar to another generation, a son who had been led to dedicate his life in the service of God meets his mother in her old age, and in their intimate talk he inquires about her hope, her outlook, her religion. "The biggest hope I've ever had," she said, "was to bear a chile that would love everybody as yer father loved me." [10] Mary of Nazareth dreamed a loftier dream than that, that her first-born would be God's promised One to the race and to the world. It was her hope that he would love men as God had loved her. When he had grown to manhood and recalled the time he had leaned on his mother's knee, is it any wonder that he regarded her as his guardian angel, and made him say with deep emotion, "For I say unto you, That in heaven their angels do always behold the face of my Father which is in heaven"? Living with Mary, the "blessed among women," [11] he must have felt as though he had stepped within the circle of the radiant love of God. Looking into the eyes of his mother he looked into the eyes of God.

If we have made much of the influence of mother-love upon the growing mind and soul of Jesus, we have made too little of three other influences. First, the carpenter Joseph. We know little about him. Only a sweet echo steals through the mist of silence that floats across his life. But he was the father in the home, and if Jesus eschewed all other names of God such as King of Kings, and Lord of Lords, may it not be that all that was contained in the human word "father" when he addressed Joseph was enough for him when he thought of God? What was Joseph but a father in a poor and humble home who spent himself in love, gave tenderly and ungrudgingly to his children? Listen in on several occasions when Jesus is talking about God and see if one cannot discover a Being of self-expenditure: "And he said unto them, Which of you shall have a friend, and shall go unto him at midnight, and say unto him, Friend, lend me three loaves; for a friend of mine in his journey is come to me, and I have nothing to set before him? And he from within shall answer and say, Trouble me not: the door is now shut, and my children are with me in bed; I cannot rise and give thee. I say unto you, Though he will not rise and give him, because he is his friend, yet because of his importunity he will rise and give him as many as he needeth. And I say unto you, Ask, and it shall be given you; seek, and ye shall find; knock, and it shall be opened unto you." "Or what man is there of you, whom if his son ask bread, will he give him a stone? Or if he ask a fish, will he give him a serpent? If ye then, being evil, know how to give good gifts unto your children, how much more shall your Father which is in heaven give good things to them that ask him?" [12]

This was all reminiscent of the intimacy of the friendship that existed between Jesus and Joseph. They understood each other, and never was there any relaxation of confidence. Long before Jesus entered upon his lifework, Joseph had grown prematurely old, dying perhaps in penury. Doubtless, if we look into a hundred modern situations, we can see Joseph on his deathbed, the gloom deepened by the dying man's fear of hunger for his little ones, and laying the charge of caring for the family upon the shoulders of the first-born in the home. Fatherless himself, yet who dare say that in all the years that followed, Jesus was not influenced by the emotions, the thoughts, and the experiences of fatherhood as he sought to ply the role of breadwinner in that household? Out of it came the matchless prayer of the ages, laden with the memory and the eternal meaning and spirit of the human home—"Our Father who art in heaven, hallowed be thy name." All the reverence, all the awe, all the humility, with which a noble son would address a good, true father to whom he owed so much, was packed into his later years when he thought of God, "My Father is greater than I." Bread, forgiveness, loving protection from evil things, in fact the whole prayer is shot through with simplicity, humility, and love. It becomes lighted up and interpenetrated in all its infinite depth when it is placed against the background of the Nazareth home.

14

Then, too, it ought never to be forgotten that Jesus' school of experience extended beyond the narrow confines of his home and the village of Nazareth. He was not only a resident of Nazareth but of the Holy Land. It has been assumed that the little village hidden behind the hills had cut him off from intimate contact with the varied interests of contemporary Galilean life in the larger centers of population. We have allowed him to climb the hills where he could catch glimpses of the land which held the history of his race, and in imagination have seen him watching the caravans moving along the highways of Galilee. But we have detached him from the city streets "where cross the crowded ways of life," and which included in its maelstrom many diverse currents of society.

Sepphoris, the largest city of Galilee, lay only five miles from Nazareth, little more than an hour's walk, and but a half hour from the largest village, Jopha. A few biographers of Jesus mention these places, but little or nothing about their social significance in the experience of the young man from Nazareth, and George Adam Smith in the *Geography of the Holy Land* completely ignores them. Where is there a man among the older generation of our day, who, as a village boy, did not walk or run that distance and stand in large-eyed wonder as he watched the movement and listened to the voices of a city's life?

Jesus must have trod the streets of these two populous centers on frequent occasions. Sepphoris, especially, had social significance for him. Long before Jesus was born Sepphoris had figured conspicuously in Jewish life. When the Romans divided Palestine into five administrative regions, Sepphoris became the capital of Galilee. It was an important military post under Herod the Great, and after his death Judas, the flaming revolutionist, equipped an army with weapons from the royal palace in Sepphoris, and made it the center of his operations. The Romans fell upon it when Jesus was a boy, they burned it, killed many of the inhabitants, and crucified the insurrectionists.

While Jesus was growing into manhood the city was rebuilt. It was so brilliantly restored by Herod Antipas that it took the name, the Ornament of Galilee. In Jesus' day its population included Jews and foreigners, becoming more Greek than Jewish. Nazareth along with many other neighborhoods became a suburb of Sepphoris. By the time the restoration was complete Jesus had reached at least his twenty-fifth year. With a vigorous building enterprise in progress, and with a mother and six younger children to support, where but in Sepphoris might Jesus have plied his trade of carpenter? The word "carpenter" in the years of Jesus meant, not only a worker in wood, but one who labored at the building trade in general. It requires no daring flight of imagination to see the youthful Jesus finding employment in Sepphoris.

But whether or not that is so, who can doubt that he found his way into the city on numerous occasions? We understand him better as we consider certain traits in his character, when we assume that his contacts were wider than the narrow limits of a secluded village. "The unconventionality of Jesus in mingling freely with the common people, his generosity toward the stranger and the outcast, and his conviction of the equality of all classes before God, perhaps owe their origin in no slight degree to the proximity of Nazareth to Sepphoris. Had Jesus spent his youth exclusively in a small village with strictly Jewish surroundings, he would have been less likely to acquire the generous attitude which later characterized his public career. But if in Sepphoris he had come into contact, or if only on brief but numerous visits to the city he frequently encountered a mixed population in the streets and in the shops, and thus grew to freedom of intercourse, we can a little better understand the genesis of that spirit of toleration which caused him to be called the 'friend of publicans and sinners.' " [13]

But if we should omit a third great influence toward the growing consciousness of God in his life, we should not understand the keenness of his intellect, and the spiritual insight which he manifested on numerous occasions and which forever made him the hope of a distracted and disordered world. He lived in a time of tension. The Jewish nationalists and the Herodians were wrestling with the problem of existence. How could the race escape annihilation? Israel was not without its powerful leaders, all of whom opposed resistance to Rome. On the one hand stood those who would have welcomed the universal Roman civilization. Greco-Roman culture was their ideal. To be a gentleman meant to be a Roman. To be sure, they had a religion which was different from that of Rome, but it was a formal religion stripped of vitality and conviction such as possessed the minds and spirits of their prophets. What difference did the religion of the upper classes of Israel make in the prospect of accepting the proposal of Rome to assimilate Israel and thus make it part of a growing, expanding empire?

On the other hand bulked that numerous and significant class to which Josephus belonged, who wanted no war with Rome. These people did not love the Roman yoke, and would have been glad to follow a leader in violent resistance, save that they saw clearly what resistance implied and foreboded. Rebellion was far beyond their physical capacity, whose inevitable result would be destruction and devastation. They loved Rome less because they could not fight, and they hated her the more. They looked at Rome with a glaring eye, and a

18

heart full of hate, but they did not dare to strike. "I endeavored," says Josephus, "to put a stop to the tumultuous persons and persuaded them to change their minds . . . and told them that they were inferior to the Romans not only in martial skill, but also in good fortune. . . . I foresaw that the end of war would be most unfortunate for us." [14]

Here in the midst of this growing tension bordering on hysteria as is indicated in the eschatological literature of the day and by the prevalence of nervous maladies, Jesus had to preach and teach. It was not unlike the hysteria of our day which has gripped the minds, not only of people in pews of churches, but in pulpits and among religious leaders who have thought more about what the Church has laid down in creed and dogma than about what possessed the mind and soul of Jesus as he looked out upon the common popular solutions of the perplexing problems of his day. Historically speaking the situation was a local problem, and religiously it was decidedly provincial. But one thing is sure: the insight of Jesus has become the most universal achievement in the long history of mankind. If Jesus had thought as did the religious leaders of his time, there would have been no teachings of Jesus and no Christian church.

It was the crisis of his time that helped make Jesus great. As Simkovitch says, "There should be nothing mystical about the trite observation that every crisis produces its great man. The fact is that under ordinary conditions of existence, when we are quite sane and safe, we are using but a small portion of our potential intellectual and emotional powers. . . . A crisis, while greatly increasing numerically the broad base of the intellectually and emotionally active members of society, quickens as well the activities of the individual, and further heightens the individual lives through their manifold interreactions. . . . Creative ability is enlarged; destructive folly is enlarged; all human activities, all elements of friction are increased for good or for evil; and the scale must be larger for the outstanding personalities who are to marshal the enlarged forces of life." [15]

When one realizes the desperate external situation in which Jesus was cast, and in imagination hears the cry of the many souls seeking for a way out and instinctively looking up toward some light and life, can anyone say that Jesus was wrong either emotionally or intellectually in his approach to the problems? Has the Church ever wanted to take out of the Gospel record the words of Luke, "To give light to those who sit in darkness and in the shadow of death, to guide our feet into the way of peace," [16] or the account of the Temptation whether it occurred within a given period of forty days and nights or whether it was a continued parable of political and religious choices? Our churches and our whole civilization would indeed be poor were they to omit the reading of these upon the occasions of the two great seasons of the church year, Christmas and Lent.

But the last word has not been said. If Jesus refused to resist Rome it was not because he would water down the great Shema, "Hear, O Israel, the Lord our God, the Lord is One," with Roman culture, or because it was expedient not to resist, even with hatred in one's heart. It was because a far higher word came to him on the fiery wings of exaltation while he kept those trysts with his Father in the silences of the night: "Ye have heard that it hath been said, Thou shalt love thy neighbour, and hate thine enemy. But I say unto you, Love your enemies, bless them that curse you, do good to them that hate you, and pray for them which despitefully use you, and persecute you; that ye may be the children of your Father which is in heaven: for he maketh his sun rise on the evil and on the good, and sendeth rain on the just and on the unjust." [17]

Can anyone say that Jesus did not resent Roman aggression as did his compatriots? Was there no national pride in his breast? Was he God masquerading as a man and telling us poor mortals that the only way we can achieve anything is by way of expediency and subterfuge; that we can never rid ourselves of pride and lust, and that human history can never be redeemed? Is that to be the message of the Church?

21

Or dare we say that whatever of national and personal pride there was in Jesus, had been subdued to humility of spirit, a new insight won, and the simple meaning of the hidden things of God revealed? Was he set down upon this round earth all ready made up, or did he achieve Godlikeness through an inner experience so deep, so vast, so compelling, that he was entitled to say to the lost sheep of the House of Israel: "Come unto me, all ye that labour and are heavy laden, and I will give you rest. Take my yoke upon you, and learn of me; for I am meek and lowly in heart: and ye shall find rest unto your souls. For my yoke is easy, and my burden is light." [18]

Spiritual insight, discernment and obedience to the highest laws of the universe and of God are not overnight achievements. But they must start somewhere. Where is there a man among us, born and cradled in a home where religious nurture was the order of the day, who has achieved the least growth in "wisdom and in stature and in favor with God and man," does not recall when as a lad of twelve or fourteen years he stood at the altar on Confirmation day and looked up into the face of the minister and vowed to remember Jesus Christ? He did not know the height and depth, the length and breadth, of the love of God, but something whispered in his ear that he was a child of God with potentialities of growth "till we all come . . . unto a perfect man, unto the measure of the stature of the fulness of Christ." [19]

It must have been so with Jesus. When, according to custom, his father and mother took him up to Jerusalem at the age of twelve to visit the shrine of his people's faith, with all the excitement of preparation, the questioning and guessing, the joy of travel, the pilgrim songs as they went, the first sight of the Holy City, who can doubt that this was a spiritual crisis that would be remembered till the day he hung on the Cross on sunbaked Calvary? All the piety of the Nazareth home, all the knowledge of his ancestral faith he had gained in the school of the Rabbis, all the emotion that the hills and stars above his village home had stirred in his breast, were fused into a personal experience as he stood in the Temple, felt his aloneness with God, and uttered the words, "My Father." It was the great word for which God was waiting to hear from the lips of all his children from the beginning of time. It was the one word which marked a perfect communion between God and man.

All that is learned from the Gospel record is that he was not with the company when they left the city. But the question that the struggling soul must ask as he reads the story is, Why? Why did he spend a whole night alone in the great city? Perhaps it was the loneliest night he had ever had. But it was a loneliness unaccompanied by fear. How else are we to answer to the

questioning of our hearts except to say that preoccupa-
tion with something mysterious and awesome kept him
from noticing the departure of the pilgrim band for
Galilee? Here he was at home in the great House of
God, and here his soul melted into the soul of his
Father. Does not the answer to his parents make that
clear? When the little company were pitching their
tents that night beyond Bethel, one sees the young lad
making his way to the now deserted camping ground
outside the city wall. Was it Olivet, or was it Gethsemane where years later he would pray, "Let this cup
pass from me"? Do we not sometimes repair to the
scenes of our childhood, or in times of crisis, to the
sacred shrines where once our emotions were stirred?

One can see this lad of twelve lying down there beneath some aged tree, wrapped about in the eerie hush
of night, and with the Pascal moon and the glistening
stars looking down upon his solitary bed. The experience in the Temple courts now became a vision. His
fathers' God was stooping over him, and for the first
time he heard as clearly as the tones of a cathedral bell,
the word to which he repeatedly turned in all his life's
decisions, "Thou art my Son." It was no more a vain
imagining than the event at the Jordan banks eighteen
years later when he listened to the call of God to come
to the aid of humanity's need and sorrow; no more than
the experience on the Mount of Transfiguration when

he looked into the face of God and the prophets, and bravely faced the first full, shuddering vision of the Cross. Here was the intimate and friendly word of God in his soul dispelling fear and terror as he remembered the words of the Psalmist: "Thou art my son; this day have I begotten thee." [20] One may hear him reply in the language of another hymn, "When I consider thy heavens, the work of thy fingers, the moon and the stars, which thou hast ordained; what is man, that thou art mindful of him? and the son of man, that thou visitest him?" [21] This was the day-dawn in his young life, and this was the light that had been gathering on the horizon of the child's mind, and now began to spread and break over all his life's sky.

There was nothing here of any metaphysical nature, nothing that brought to his mind a pretemporal state. His way of drawing near to his Father was spiritual and moral. He climbed the ladder to God on the rungs of trust, surrender and love. Did he know his destiny? Did he see the Cross? Did he feel the kiss of Judas? Did he hear himself denounced as some strange usurper of Caesar's crown? There is nothing in the record to indicate anything of this sort, only a desire to venture upon the truth of God, and to give his life to God to do with it whatever seemed good, and to recognize the divine authority. This filial relation produced in him a feeling that he had a work to do in the world, some amends to

make for the long dearth of human love to God, a commission from God to make a fresh offer from God who
had agonized from the beginning over the estrangement
between him and mankind.

That this was the precise pathway by which the young
soul of Jesus traveled toward its God may not be literally
true. Knowing something, however, of the manner in
which we ourselves have climbed into the sacred pre-
cincts of the soul of God, we must say it is true in its
main contention. As a boy of twelve he had gained a
clear sense of the presence of God, and when he stood
in the waters of the Jordan he rounded out whatever
may have been inarticulate in the Temple. He saw the
outline of what his vocation should be, and as he trod
the country lanes, ate his bread in sorrow and saw the
multitudes wandering about as sheep without a shepherd, his sense of mission deepened and grew more intense, until it rose in sharper outline on the Mount of
Transfiguration, at Caesarea Philippi, and on the white
ribbon of road on the way to the Cross in Jerusalem. It
was a God-consciousness in the Temple, a heaven-sent
commission at the Baptism, and on the slopes of Mt.
Hermon a service of sorrow and death in behalf of God's
growing children. In the end it could be nothing more
or less than becoming "obedient unto death, even the
death of the cross." [22]

II

How His Soul Stood at Ease Before God

IT SEEMS almost profane to search out with curious eyes the hidden secret that lay back of Jesus' intimacy with God. There are books in my library that reveal the wrestling, the stammering, the straining, of the author in his attempt to tell the story of the inward road he himself has traveled toward the vision he has seen. As one reads one begins to wonder how clear is the vision and whether the very incoherence of the language is not indicative of the obscurity of the vision. It was not so with Jesus.

There was little sign of the introspective in his utterances. Someone said long ago that the painting of an artist ought to give the impression that it was done easily and spontaneously. When one catches a glimpse of Jesus as he talked with the doctors and lawyers in the Temple, and later listens in to the conversation with the woman at Jacob's well, or sees him sitting on the hillside and hears him say, "Blessed are the pure in spirit, for they shall see God," one sees a soul so un-divided, so simple, so sure of its faith, that one concludes he must have come by these insights naturally and spontaneously.

When the ecclesiastical officials chided the people for not bringing Jesus to them for condemnation, they replied, "Never man spake like this man." [1] When folk went home after watching and hearing him for a day, some reported to their families, "We never saw it on this fashion." [2] Others said, "We have seen strange things today." [3] Never man spake so clearly, and never man conveyed so simply what he saw, as did Jesus. He is the supreme illustration of the union of vision and simplicity. Saints of all ages have told us of their peculiar psychic experiences in their desire to stand in the presence of God, of their wrestlings and their ecstasies, and how their hearts were strangely warmed. But no word of such experiences escaped the lips of Jesus. He had his vigils, he sought the reassurance of his Father in the silence of the wilderness, and he returned to his task refreshed after long nights of prayer. One would like to know what transpired between him and his Father on those occasions. But a veil is drawn over them, and when he speaks he does not tell us, and we marvel at the objectivity of his speech. One feels, however, that the landscape of his thought was swept clear and bare of abstractions and God stood out in clear outline before his hearers.

"His very paradoxes and aphorisms are not dim opals, and rubies, and pearls of fantasy, but clear sparkling stones of reason and conscience. His parables and similitudes are tender and homelike flowers of imagination." [4]

Often, as a young lad, and as a growing youth, I asked my soul, as I sat in church, "Why must the face of God be made so obscure in pulpit and in ritual?" This must be the cry of many hungry souls as they wait before a Gospel, the main business of which should concern the human soul. Why should not the vision of God be as natural as breathing, as full of sweet and obvious reasonableness as the air is full of sunlight?

I find myself wishing that we could rid ourselves of the fable, the myth, the false emphasis upon, and interpretation of, the Gospel which has so hindered the triumphant march of Christianity through the world, and without prejudice or preconceived notions, open once again the record of the Master's life with all the amazing clearness and simplicity in his words. What a difference it would make to the men and women in their dim-eyed fumbling and groping after reality! After all, the final test of any religion is its inherent spiritual dynamic. Religion is not a school of morals, not a system of speculation, but an enthusiasm. Humanity does not need morals, it needs motives; it is weary of speculation and longs for action. The crown and destiny of all things in the universe and out of it, and the gateway to the supreme vision of God is found where Browning found it, in

> That one Face, far from vanish, rather grows,
> Or decomposes but to recompose,
> Become my universe that feels and knows!

The bedrock upon which one can build a superstructure which rises toward the mountain peaks where one can behold the reality which responds and communes with the individual soul, is found in the qualities of the heart: humility, purity and love. They were the crowning attributes of the life of Jesus, and are no different in common mortals than they were in him. The thing that gives them validity and makes them the controlling factors of life, is to see them from God's point of view.

Jesus was the humblest man who ever lived. As he grew to manhood and left his childhood behind him, he never broke with childlikeness. It is not the childish mind that enters the Kingdom, but the childlike mind, the "teachable, and aspiring, who compare themselves with the loftiest ideals and know they have not attained their highest, and who feel that the power by which they do their best work is given to them, not created by them. It is to such that even the world says 'Come up higher.' " [5] Jesus chose the humble life because it was consistent with his plan, because it would produce a finished and artistic life, and because it was in reality the means of the fullest success. It was not strange that Paul, when wishing to appeal to his brethren by that which was most unique and compelling in the character of Jesus, should say, "I . . . beseech you by the meekness and gentleness of Christ." [6] Jesus said, "Thou hast hid these things from the wise and prudent, and hast revealed them unto babes," [7] and in the next breath claimed that "All things are delivered unto me of my Father," [8] and then sets himself among the lowliest of men with the words, "I am meek and lowly in heart." [9] He knew that all great things of life are simple, and they can be grasped only by simplicity.

When Jesus holds a little child before one's gaze and bids one be like him, one has a right to lay claim to the idea of original goodness as well as to the idea of original sin. In a little child there is the absence of self-consciousness and complete absorption in what comes flooding into him from without. To be sure, the child is often the archegotist who insists that all things must minister to his desires. But when Jesus talked about the humility of a little child, he was thinking of how the child recognizes external facts, and the open-eyed wonder with which he looks upon nature. It smacks of the manner in which my little grandson stood on the threshold of the Eternal one day when he said to me in the garden, "The earth is full of God's riches, isn't it?" It was the mystic consciousness of the child-heart that possessed Jesus. All nature, all men and all children are instinct with God.

The humble heart listens and receives. Humility hears God whisper, "My Son," and replies with utmost trust, "God stoops to me." Pride vanishes, and as one looks up to the towering heights of God's majesty one feels one's intimacy with God, and finds oneself saying with Jesus, "My Father rules, and the earth is his footstool." [10]

When Jesus asked, "Why callest thou me good? There is none good but One—God," [11] he was not toying with his emotions, a sure sign of self-preoccupation. His was the humility of a man who felt that what he was came from God, that he was linked forever with the Eternal, and that what was communicated between himself and his Father was as real as the intimacy between a trusting daughter and an understanding mother. The same voice that called him "Son" was the word that controlled the forces of the universe. This was the manner of his entrance into the Kingdom, a childlike trust and a childlike receiving of God's spirit.

Where else could this lead him but to an intense and far-flung vision of God to whom all things are possible? Everything in the universe moved in rhythmic fashion under the controlling power of God. The only disharmony he saw about him was in the human will, and so long as the human heart failed to respond there could be no cosmic harmony, and the will of God could not be done on earth as it is in heaven. When spiritual perspective goes, when men allow the sanctity of God's law to fade out, and prefer to follow the small traditions and the unethical man-made precepts by which to guide the destiny of nations, then the Kingdom of God is an infinitely remote accomplishment.

The great human tragedy in Jesus' mind is the attempt of men to preserve the gift of freedom on every other basis than that of obedience to divine law. The fears which men had in his day, and the fear which a so-called Christian nation such as ours has today, of losing its freedom at the hands of some Godless nation, is nothing compared to the greatest fear of all: that the soul of a man and a nation can be cast away in death. "Fear him, which after he hath killed hath power to cast into hell. . . . Fear him." [12] The amazing and most appealing thing, however, in all the teachings of Jesus, is that he believed in the freedom of the human will. He never forced himself upon man's will. He saw a condescending, wistful and eager God, calling upon men to accept his will, and setting before them the way of life and the way of death. "Even so it is not the will of your Father which is in heaven, that one of these little ones should perish." [13]

As he was humble, so he was pure. Only a pure heart could have said, "Blessed are the pure in heart; for they shall see God." [14] Purity shone in his eyes and into the

hearts around him. There is nothing in his life to indi-
cate that there ever was a time when he did not love
God with his whole body, soul and mind. As Adolph
Harnack said, "There lie behind the public ministry of
Jesus no painful crisis and tumults, no break with his
past." [15] John Masefield could make Saul Kane exclaim:

> O glory of the lighted mind,
> How dead I'd been, how dumb, how blind! [16]

and the Old Skeptic could be made to say:

> I will go back and believe in the deep old foolish tales,
> And pray the simple prayers that I learned at my mother's
> knee,
> Where the Sabbath tolls its peace through the breathless
> mountain-vales,
> And the sunset's evening hymn hallows the listening
> sea.[17]

But no such desert of deep contrition is found in
Jesus. From a winsome, innocent lad he passed into
mature manhood, carrying no scars of struggle, and with
no sense of penitence. God and the world around him
were his home. The five physical senses which are ours
were his also. Without them he would have been incomplete. They were the doors that led to his inner life, each
of which was kept open by a pure heart and the spirit of

forgiveness. Everything about him throbbed and tingled with purity, and all nature and all life were instinct with holiness, yearning and eagerness. Theologians have sneered at Albert Schweitzer's reverence for life, but where did he learn it but from Jesus of Nazareth, to whom not even the least and meanest thing was beyond an all-pervading knowledge. God notes the fall of a sparrow, and he has numbered the hairs of a man's head. The deeds of men are registered somewhere, their thoughts and needs noted. If this were not true only hopelessness and despair would be the lot of any man who enters his secret closet to pray to the God who sees in secret and rewards openly. To Jesus, God was omniscient and pervaded life everywhere as light does the atmosphere.

What other than love is born out of a humble and pure heart? The word "sinless" does not adequately describe the character of Jesus. One could wish that this word could be stricken from our vocabulary when we think of him. What he had was a concentration of purpose, and into such a life no deflection from the course which led more and more unto the perfect day could come. Love was more to him than "the expulsive power of a new affection," in Jonathan Edward's phrase; it was the defensive fortress that kept out the evils that could destroy his soul. The idea of a Kingdom wherein dwelleth righteousness took complete possession of him and swept him along like a torrent. In such a mind, as Victor Hugo said, "an unworthy thought can no more spring up than a nettle upon a glacier."

Let us not set Jesus on a pinnacle and remove him from the sphere of our common struggle toward achieving the highest perfection in the art of living. Ask the artist the secret of his art, he will not tell you it is his technique. He will say, "My art is my love of beauty, it is my belief in beauty; it is awareness that beauty is the soul of the material universe. I find beauty everywhere." Ask the saint what path he walked until he found himself in the presence of God, he will answer, "I looked into my heart. When I discovered that my interests in life were not devoted solely to the contemplation of myself and my needs, my aches and my pains, my joys and my sadnesses; when I discovered that I was going out more and more to people, that I found in men and women and little children something that satisfied me, then the fact of God became a reality. My feeling toward people and my joy in them were greater than my indifference and contempt of them, and there God became real. I was partner with that in the universe which wells up in me as love."

What other was it in Jesus than this getting out of himself, this profound respect for personality, that propelled him in the direction of love, not only for a particular class of men, but for all men? It is found in his burning chivalry in defense of the helpless that brought the hot words to his lips, "But whoso shall offend one of these little ones which believe in me, it were better for him that a millstone were hanged about his neck, and that he were drowned in the depth of the sea." [18] It is found in his passionate longing to be the protector of the multitudes from the evil forces that were abroad, even as a shepherd guards his sheep; in that confession of love that would spread itself like protecting wings around his beloved Jerusalem; in the scorn that he showed for those who would stone the prophets, and in the prayer that he uttered in behalf of his enemies as they drove the nails through his hands and feet.

> . . . but true love never yet
> Was thus constrained it overleaps all fence;
> Like lightning, with invisible violence
> Piercing its continents; like Heaven's free breath,
> Which he who grasps can hold not; like death,
> Who rides upon a thought, and makes his way
> Through temple, tower, and palace and the array
> Of arms; more strength has Love than he or they;
> For he can burst his charnel, and make free
> The limbs in chains, the heart in agony,
> The soul in dust and chaos.[19]

Even when he was a boy his loving heart looked out upon nature and saw it transfused with love and power.

The lilies of the field told him that God in his majesty had passed that way. The wind as it sighed through the boughs of the tree or as it shook the reeds by the river was the sound of his Father's going. The crimson sky of the evening spoke of God's promises. The rain and the sunshine were God's largesse upon the otherwise fruitless soil. Flowers and birds appeared as God's creative joy, and when he saw the lair of the fox and the nest of the bird, he knew that it is not God's desire that there be a homeless creature in the world. The bleat of the lost sheep told him of stupid humanity that nibbles at this little tuft of grass, and drinks from this little running stream of material satisfaction, until it gets caught in the thicket of compromise, subterfuge and the holocaust of war. The dismal howling of the pariah dogs sounded in his ears like the anguish of human beings in eternal pain. The hen gathering her brood under her wings made him cry.[20]

All of this is found in the poet's soul. And Jesus was a poet, not merely a rhymer and a musician, but a revelation of God that flowed through him and spoke in language that the common man could understand. His words in their beauty and simplicity, uttered from a compassionate human heart, told his hearers that he carried within himself the great, brooding, yearning secrets of the universe, and that the heart of Reality is love, and love is of God. To us who find ourselves so often missing the way and coming to our wits' end, that great refrain which recurs among the Parables of lost things: "There is joy in the presence of the angels of God over one sinner that repenteth," [21] is the loveliest of lovely glimpses of Jesus' vision of God. It reminds us of the scene of creation as depicted in the drama of Job. When God had finished his work and looked on it and saw that it was good, the "morning stars sang together, and all the sons of God shouted for joy." [22] So here, the face of God is wreathed in smiles as he points to one returning prodigal, and the angels burst into a song of rapturous joy.

Until the Church sees Jesus in his selfless love fighting his way through the barriers of human fear, pride and despair which he saw in the social life about him, and finding his life in sharing the very need and misery of man, it will go on resting its case for existence upon so many churches, so many members, so much money. It is only when a man loves the whole world, not only his friends but his enemies, that the world becomes transfused and illumined, and he sees at the heart of it the presence of God. It is then that he knows that love is the only attribute that fully and completely fits the personality of Jesus. He shall not miss out in his case for Jesus Christ if he casts away much that theology, creed and dogma have woven about him, but he shall be poor indeed if he fails to see and declare his self-identification of his love with its object and its eternal source. "Whoever receives this little child in my name receives me, and whoever receives me receives him who sent me. For it is the lowliest of you all who is great." [23]

These qualities—humility, purity and love—take nothing away from the intellectual ability of Jesus. But it was from them that his mind took its flight, quickened his imagination, and gave him immediate conclusion on the vexing problems of life. He spoke in pictures, in parables, in epigram and in paradox, not in long-drawn-out systems of thought. He comes to the point quickly and the truth shines out crystal clear. He breaks through the rules of strict logic, yet his teaching was more than analogy and similitude. It was a breaking off of the fragments and the manifestation of the mind and spirit of God. He saw clearly and he was bent on making people see things as he saw them, hear things as he heard them, and feel their spiritual value and significance, their dignity as human beings, even before he asked them to think things out. He believed that people were possessed with spiritual capacity—some more, some less—to respond to the touch which his insight made clear.

His religious philosophy was not a plaything to be juggled about, nor to be dangled at the end of a series of intellectual gymnastics. He never dealt in arguments in order to convince the minds of men. He was bent upon declaring a truth which could move and change the soul. He never went off at tangents. His mind was well poised because it was set in the direction of God's mind. His asking of questions was an appeal to the heart and conscience. His commands were a summons to men to use their moral sense. When he said, "Consider the lilies," he was not telling people merely to look at a garden. He was saying that a man who could look at this creation of God with awe and wonder had achieved some moral value. No evil mind could consider a lily or anything else of beauty. But if a man starts out to do the will of God he "shall know of the doctrine, whether it be of God, or whether I speak of myself." [24] It is only when life is quiet, when the egocentric will becomes the divine will, does God speak. It was this losing of himself in the soul of God that lifted the reason of Jesus to the place of vision, and which sent him out with urgent action into the world of men. The intellect of Jesus did not show itself in formal thought, but in practical life situations. When the angel appeared to the shepherds on the hills of Judea he carried a message of Good News to all the world. "Behold, I bring you good tidings of great joy." [25] It was this knowledge of the Good Will, the Good News, the Glad Tidings, of God, that gave thought to his teachings, and made the people exclaim, "This man speaks with authority and not as the scribes." [26]

Marvelous was the manner in which he sought to appeal to the best, not the worst, in human nature! He did not go about telling people that they were vile sinners, but that they had their values confused. Keeping the Sabbath law was important, but when a man pitied a sheep that had fallen into the pit on the Sabbath, he was seeing a living thing as God saw it. A blade of grass is frail and fragile under the foot of a vacationist, but rightly seen it is a miracle, more resplendent than all the pomp and glory of Solomon's court. A sparrow might be cheap, but it was God's creation. It took as much ingenuity for God to create it as to set the sun, moon and stars in their places. And if a sparrow was important, what about a man? "You are of more value than many sparrows."

God is interested in grass and sheep, but much more in a man. Is a man's life merely that of a beast nibbling grass? Is not the true nature of man to be found in the fact that he hungers and thirsts after righteousness? The true man is the man who can show tenderness to these lower forms of creation for the simple reason that it is a manifestation of something divine that has flooded his soul.

When Blaise Pascal said, "Man is a reed, the weakest in nature, but he is a thinking reed," [27] and of more abiding worth than anything that may crush him, he was re-echoing the sublime insight of Jesus: "What shall it profit a man if he gain the whole world, and lose his own soul? Or what shall a man give in exchange for his soul?" The chief thing about a man is that he belongs to God. He can will himself out of the life of God, but nothing else can, not even death, because God is the God of the living and not of the dead.

The cry of the human soul down through the ages has ever been, What is God like? When Jesus wants to show what God is like he seizes upon one of the holiest facts in human life—the love of a father and mother—and says that God can be no less noble than that of a parent in his purest affection and love. "What man is there of you, who, if his son ask bread, will give him a stone? . . . If ye then, being evil, know how to give good gifts unto your children, how much more shall your Father which is in heaven give good things to them that ask him?" [28] Is there anything in this changing life that can outlast the love of a father and mother? Will the shame of the far country wear out the father's love for the prodigal? When he said, "ye being evil," he knew the shortcomings of parents, their failures and follies, their unkindness at times, their misunderstanding of children, their proneness to precept rather than example. He saw these as clearly as he saw the grave limits to human nature everywhere.

Yet the instinct of parenthood survives. If you can take love and set it down in the midst of a city's slum district, or where squalor and filth and beastliness have marred the pure image of God in human life, and make it live on, never crushed or unquenched in the most sordid environment, what other can one say than that its source is found in God who says, "Though your sins be as scarlet, they shall be as white as snow; though they be red like crimson, they shall be as wool"? [29] Anyone who has given himself to the re-creation not only of a human being, but of his environment, knows that God is far more noble than he, and that the gifts he has provided for mankind are of greater value than any his children can offer. We may grow weary, disheartened and discouraged, but "the Creator of the ends of the earth, fainteth not, neither is weary. . . . He giveth power to the faint; and to them that have no might he increaseth strength." [30] God is the Father pouring himself out in endless service and sacrifice for men.

Does this belittle God? Is there nothing in this imperial soul of man that is worthy of being called similar to the character of God? Is God too vast, too awful, too unknowable, that one should dare to think that not only is man made in the image of God, but that God also is made in the image of man? If this human analogy is not valid, then nothing human is valid—no thought, no deed, no holding out of hands of mercy to a wayward soul, no deep longing, no sighing, no heart-rending cry for forgiveness. God becomes an ogre who flung man down upon this earth and at whose caprice can be saved or damned for God's glory. Then the noblest word that was ever uttered, "Father," becomes an anachronism, and in whose bosom no storm-swept soul would ever wish to find refuge.

"He is most beautiful and wise,
He dwelleth in the moisty skies,
In the grey wall at heaven's rim,
And he has made me after him."

Then laughed I in superior mirth,
"Attend, ye creatures of the earth,
Misled, mistaken, all undone
And self-deceivers, every one.

"Hear ye, deluded beasts, while I
Explain the shape God wears, and why.
Self-evident the truth's displayed:
He is my Father, sirs," I said,
"And in my image He is made!" [31]

But Jesus possessed something more than intellect which gave him keen insight into the problems of human beings, and how to deal with them. He saw the doors of new life opening to men in a new realm, the realm of God which he brought with him into the world. It was the first message he carried into Galilee after standing with John at the Jordan. The time has now come, God's reign is near: repent—change your mind—and believe in the Gospel.

There is enough in the petition of Jesus, "Thy kingdom come, thy will be done on earth as it is in heaven," to keep one writing long after this chapter comes to an end. It seems so natural and so sane that he should be talking about a condition of life here on earth that would be touched with heaven's breath. He did not define it, he only drew a series of immortal pictures. It would not come through violent upheavals, or paroxysms, or miraculous intervention. Men would not need to look for "signs." It would come as gently and simply as daylight, or as flowers and grass spring out of the soil. "The kingdom of God cometh not with observation: neither shall they say, Lo here! or, lo there! for, behold, the kingdom of God is within you." [32] Men do not need to look up into the sky, nor imagine it is coming with every changing fashion of society. There would be no cataclysm in earth or sky in response to the prayers or the seeking of men. It will come as the day succeeds day, each one with the same hope, the same wonders, and the same longings of the heart. A blade of grass comes, then the ear, then the full corn, until at last before our amazed eyes a ripe field lies outspread. The Kingdom is at hand!

The manner of its coming is that of a tiny mustard seed growing into a wide-spreading tree. "It is a waking of the better self, a breath of awe, a gust of holy joy, a faint impulse of faith—present to the soul for a moment, then hidden in the garden of memory. Yet, because it is a living thing, it is destined to germinate and become a mighty tree, visited by winged fancies from the spiritual world, and melodious with voices of rapture and praise. Or, it may begin in some hidden but constant unrest, some ferment of soul, some heartache, or mental anguish. Not till the great testing occasion, the high summons to action comes, do we realize what is taking place: the kingdom has leavened the whole lump." [33]

Yet, for all of its naturalness, there will be times of sudden and glad surprise. Even though one lives in the midst of the commonplace and life becomes decidedly monotonous, the wonders of the Kingdom will break at times and one will stumble upon some great treasure. Then values will be changed, and with new light dawning in the soul where consecration to the highest one knows becomes the end of one's living, and every common bush will be aflame with God. When that time comes one will not count the cost. Religion will move out of the place where doing the will of God is no longer duty but sheer happiness. The disciples left all and followed eagerly. Paul yielded up without any regret his Pharisaic birth and learning: "But what things were gain to me, I counted loss for Christ." [34] Augustine parted with his darling sins because "What I feared to be parted from was now a joy to surrender. For thou didst cast them forth from me, Thou true and high sweetness. Thou didst cast them forth, and in their

place didst enter in thyself, sweeter than all pleasure." [35]
For the Kingdom of God, this thing of infinite depth
and worth, to become the posession of man, all the
experience of a lifetime is not too big a price to pay.

In all the parables of the Kingdom of God, Jesus was
but revealing his own experiences. There is no sudden
upheaval in his life, but day by day new light broke upon
his path. Moments came to him when he received fresh
truth from God, when the full tide of the healing waters
of God's love flooded his spirit. Whenever these moments came his spirit leaped to answer the vision, and
he abandoned himself to the leading and direction of
each new disclosure of God. That is why, when he is
seen in the middle of his ministry, doing the will of God
had become natural to him, and men saw in him the
God who walked the earth and shared the sins, the sorrows, the disappointments and the tears of his children.

There can be no doubt that at times Jesus saw a Kingdom where men should "do justly, love mercy, and walk
humbly before God." When he looked about and saw
the few minds and hearts that had begun to be in the
grip of an eternal truth, might it not be that this was
evidence of the coming Kingdom? But the disappointing thing to any man who sees a great truth surging and
straining to break in and flood the world with something
new, fresh and vital is the hard hearts and the obtuse
minds of men. It was so with Jesus. His spirits drooped,

but the vision never faded, and his confidence that God could yet breathe upon the dry bones and requicken the world never forsook him. When the disciples returned to him with marvelous tales of the success of their preaching, he rejoiced in spirit, and when they wondered at the radiance which lit up his face, he said, "I beheld Satan as lightning fall from heaven." [36] Here we may say that he fell back upon the apocalyptic imagery so prevalent in his day. Even so, without his belief that one day the word would not return unto him void, but would accomplish that which God pleased and prosper in the thing whereto it was sent, he could scarcely have persisted until the dark night of Calvary closed about him.

It is frequently said that Jesus was a visionary. I listened one Sunday morning to a bright middle-aged preacher telling the congregation that Jesus was an idealist: to follow him would mean that we had to eat as he ate, dress as he dressed, give up our occupations and professions and go about as itinerant preachers. I wondered how many of us fall back upon calling Jesus an idealist as an excuse for our unwillingness to measure the mind of God in areas where the lives and souls of men are at stake. For to call Jesus an idealist, and an impractical dreamer, is to misunderstand the laws of God and the universe, and to make of Jesus a mere symbol of Christianity and of God a negative quantity.

It ought to be remembered that not only in Communist countries does Christianity face opposition. It is equally true in non-Communist countries where not only is the number of active church members a pitiably small minority of the population, but many people who do attend church repudiate the teachings of Jesus as a practical solution of the world's vexing problems.

Jesus was the world's supreme realist. He would never have died for anything that was impossible of achievement. He would have refused to become absorbed in anything that would perish with his death. He saw everything against the background of God in an orderly universe, and knew for a certainty that the true destiny of a man, a nation and the world is found only when the discord and strife are lost in the nobler symphony of unity with the eternal life of the Spirit.

This is quite different from the modern thought of realism which makes its compromises with materialism, accommodates itself so neatly to the evil of the world, and imagines that mankind can retain a desire for the things of God, and at the same time be so reluctant to let go of the protective coloration of the society in which we live. "Ye cannot serve God and mammon," for it is clear that the light of God will go out of the heart of a man, a nation and a church that is divided and distracted. "The light of the body is the eye: if therefore thine eye be single, thy whole body shall be full of light.

But if thine eye be evil, thy whole body shall be full of darkness, how great is that darkness!" [37]

To Jesus there was no meaning in the idea that the world is so desperately wicked that it is forever shut up in the dark prison house of material pursuits that it will not allow the glory of God freely to shine in. From this moral miasma which has settled down upon the mind and heart Jesus would set us free. Unless the Church is willing to take Jesus out of the moth balls of ritual and creed, and put his teachings into law offices, legislative halls, business, factories, labor unions, colleges and international relations, we shall go on giving him lip service while we watch the so-called Christian civilization tumble and fall before the gods of paganism.

To watch again the methods and purposes which Jesus pursued in his short sojourn on earth is to discover how he tried to dispel the great veil of moral illusion which hung before the eyes of men, and which shut out the life of God in the human soul. When George F. Baer, president of the Reading Railroad, wrote to a worried resident of Wilkes-Barre, Pennsylvania, during the coal strike in 1902: "The rights and interests of the laboring man will be protected and cared for—not by the labor agitators, but by the Christian men to whom God in his infinite wisdom has given control of the property interests of the country," [38] he was giving expression to one of the great illusions which prevent people from

51

seeing the world irradiated with the light of the divine life. Earthly prosperity then was, and still is, reckoned by many to be proof that a man is living in the sunshine of heaven's smile, and that God is looked upon as the great mammon and as a self-interested Being. But to Jesus the successful follower of mammon was only a rich fool, because of his short-range thinking. The only thing that could come to a man of that kind was the dissolution of a soul that had found its life in the glitter and glamour of things. Jesus saw how hard it is for a rich man to enter the Kingdom, not merely because he is rich, but because his riches stand between him and good deeds, his sense of failure to know that true enrichment is the enrichment gotten by giving, and that riches can so easily erase the line between the soul and things. Self-sacrifice, not self-assertion, is the true cosmic law, and self-sacrifice is only another name for God.

Another persistent illusion that Jesus sought to dispel was anxiety for oneself and the fear one has of tomorrow. These make the world in which man lives a haunted house. When Jesus saw the reliability of God upon which such creatures as birds and flowers depended, he told people that the same faithfulness that fed the bird, clothed the grass, kept the promise of bursting fig-tree buds, reigned everywhere, and God's care for human beings was as certain as the coming of summer. Anxiety about tomorrow made men question if there would be a tomorrow. But to him God was in tomorrow as well as in today. Even the evil in the world could not put men beyond the range of God's magnanimity.

These were not just beautifully spoken words. Jesus had tested out God's care, and he knew that God wanted people to be always dependent upon God's day-by-day care. God would never fail man's dependence, and when he would once cease his pushing for more things and more things, he should find that God's generous hand had always given good measure, pressed down, shaken together, heaped up and running over. It was poverty of spirit—the lack of desire for things—that God hoped to find. He longed to see the freedom which comes by letting go, and the joy that pervades the heart of a person who believes that God "giveth us richly all things to enjoy." [39]

Not only did Jesus stand against this secular aspect of life, but he had little patience with the religious externalism of his time. Time and again he showed how wrong the spiritual leaders were. When he looked at the Pharisees and noted how the minds and spirits of men were drawn off in the outer regions of endless meticulosity and scrupulousness, under the vain delusion that thus a man could find favor with God, he asked, "Why do ye also transgress the commandment of God by your tradition?" [40] Such distortion of religion into duty, and nothing else, is an abomination to God, and

the egocentricity which makes a man crave social standing, good reputation and flawless obedience to all formalism, he called hypocrisy. This he had to confront in
all his efforts to bring God back into human life, and to
make men see that God is spirit, a boundless energy
that puts itself at the disposal of human souls.

Whenever Jesus started out to put men on the pathway which he, himself, had trod, he was made aware of
the darkened and oppressive atmosphere which the
Pharisees had created. And with words that sometimes
burned and scorched he sought to shrivel up this garment of illusion in which the religious leaders of his day
had wrapped themselves. A religion which had gone
astray was of no value to men who would again discover
a God who was waiting with both hands full of priceless
treasure.

Nor did he want a religion of self-abasement that
found its expression in sackcloth robes, unwashed faces,
and ash-besprinkled hair. Whether these things were
done consciously or unconsciously, they were done to
win public attention. The true heart to which God made
his approach was the heart that was laid bare in the
privacy of the closet. It was there that a man should
find the tender, healing intimacy of God. Here, too,
Jesus gave us a page out of his own spiritual progress.
He never knew the remorse we know after we have
failed so miserably, or the gnawing sense of guilt. But

he knew the pain that love suffers when others suffer, and he knew the sorrow that pierced the hearts of countless sufferers about him. Those secret trysts with his Father kept him ever compassionate with the sighs and tears of his fellow men. While he mused the fire burned and the flame leaped up, as he heard the voice: "Surely he hath borne our griefs, and carried our sorrows . . . the chastisement of our peace was upon him; and with his stripes we are healed." [41]

Nor did he have any word of commendation for the self-advertising almsgiver. Against that kind he set the kindness done by stealth, that never sought approval, and the generous impulse of the right hand that could never hope to gain admiration of the left hand. "In thee I am well-pleased" is reserved for him who, out of self-concealing disinterestedness of true generosity, gives and does deeds of neighborly kindness and pity, and knows that he is only a steward of the gifts that have been put into his hand.

Still the probe of Jesus goes deeper until it reaches the place where countless numbers of God's children lie crushed beneath the relentless and pitiless external penalism which showed itself as unforgiving temper that would hide from a man even the forgiveness of God. It issued out in revenge, and called down disease, sorrow and death upon those who transgressed one tittle of the law. God was represented as an austere Being, reaping where he had not sown, and gathering where he had not strewed. The only way that Jesus had of breaking through this veil of moral delusion was to show them the God of the forgiving heart. Forgiveness does not destroy law, it transcends law. Jesus of Nazeareth who walked the country lanes and trod the city streets of Palestine did not show men a tithe-paying, precept-mongering man, but a man of mercy, who forgave his fellow men their failures and offenses against him. The earth grew fairer and friendlier where he walked. No man can follow him very far in his ministry without discovering that he was like God and because of his tender mercy had become co-partner with his Father.

This does not imply that a society founded on right-eousness and justice is built upon a false foundation, or that God can deny his holiness. Forgiveness is no milk-and-water virtue. Any man who is sensitive to wrong, and who knows the wickedness that can be done by folk who have no sense of kindness and mercy, knows how hard it is to forgive. It is not easy for God to forgive. It costs him deep pain and travail of soul. But he does forgive.

And Jesus who radiated forgiveness felt and knew what it cost God to forgive and became the incarnation of God's forgiveness. The fog of moral illusion, mammonism, care and fear, Pharisaism, the deceptions of envy and revenge, never obscured his sight. The world of men lay before his feet, and someday he believed the realm of God would appear, and men would live in the spirit of self-forgetfulness, intimate neighborliness, mercy and joy. Two thousand years have passed since he saw the vision and we have come to the place where that vision must be actualized or we shall see what an A-bombed earth looks like. We will soon have to make our decision as to whether Jesus was a dreamy sentimentalist or a realist.

III

The World a Divine-Human Brotherhood

WHERE is there a true minister who, after he has
humbly and sincerely delivered his message, has
not at one time or another been told, "That was for
me," or "Something drew me here this morning," or
"You were sent to speak that word to me"? If the message reached down to the deepest experiences of the
human soul, if it drove the mist from the mind and spirit
of the apprehending worshiper, the preacher may be
sure that the message was not given to him of himself.

Any word from the lips of a prophet spoken with sin-
cerity and conviction that sometimes stings like a serpent's fangs, or soothes like a mother's kiss; that unveils
the depth of remorse, or points to the heavenly heights
of purity and peace; that recalls the treachery of a
Judas, or reveals the loveliness of Jesus Christ, must
touch the fibers of some person's heart as if it were a
responsive instrument. Yet, where is the thinking man
who does not feel that the metaphysical walls which

have been built around Jesus by the confessional dogmas of the Church are so high and so strong, that much of what the preacher says of the true nature and spirit of Jesus fails to get in? Conformity, which is the aim of dogma and creed, has acted as an opiate in religion, dulling the spirit of adventurous search and lulling the mind into complacency.

> The good old bishops took a simpler way;
> Each ask'd but what he heard his father say,
> Or how he was instructed in his youth,
> And by tradition's force upheld the truth.[1]

Professors of systematic theology have told us ever since World War I that it is not what Jesus said and did, but what the Church says about Jesus, that constitutes Christianity. Without certain beliefs nothing that a man does or thinks can come within the range of Christian philosophy. It reminds one of how his dour Scottish relatives told Lord Tweedsmuir in his youth that Sir Walter Scott, "having neglected certain evangelical matters, was no doubt in torment." "The news," says Tweedsmuir, "gave me much satisfaction, for the prospect of such company removed from me any fear of the infernal regions." [2]

If the stranglehold which a mass of contradictory and inscrutable propositions has placed upon the free spirit of men is to be loosened, and if the haunting sug-

59

gestiveness of a man's heart is to be recovered, it is necessary to think ourselves back to the day when Jesus walked the earth, and join the people in Galilee who listened to him, and with no preconceived notions about who he was and whence he came. The Gospel of John, which no Biblical critic has yet told us for a certainty when it was written and by whom, rings the changes on the words: "I came down from heaven, not to do mine own will, but the will of him that sent me." [3] But a surer knowledge of what Jesus began to do and to teach will be gained by following the better authenticated accounts of Matthew, Mark and Luke. Any messenger of God who will take his *Harmony of the Gospels* seriously will learn a language for his mind and soul which he has never learned before.

When Matthew, the tax collector, was celebrating his call into the little circle of disciples, he made a feast to which he invited people whose reputations were no better than his own; and when it was discovered that Jesus had so flaunted the religious tradition of the scribes and the Pharisees as to sit in the midst of this motley crowd, they sneered: "How is it that he eateth and drinketh with publicans and sinners?" His answer pointed the direction of his ministry: "I came, not to call the righteous, but sinners to repentance." [4] It sounded again in the Sermon on the Mount: "Think not that I am come to destroy the law or the prophets: I

am not come to destroy, but to fulfill." [5] It is heard
when he takes to himself the word of the prophet that
day when he stood up to read in the synagogue in
Nazareth: "The Spirit of the Lord is upon me, because
he hath anointed me to preach the gospel to the poor;
he hath sent me to heal the brokenhearted, to preach
deliverance to the captives, and recovering of sight to
the blind, to set at liberty them that are bruised, to
preach the acceptable year of the Lord." [6] The same
word echoes at the close of his Galilean ministry, and
all along his weary path to the city of Jerusalem. When
his disciples in their anger at the inhospitable treatment
by the Samaritans wanted to call down fire on their
heads, he said, "The Son of man is not come to destroy
men's lives, but to save them." [7] In that never-to-be-
forgotten scene in the home of Zacchaeus, one can hear
the throbbing tenderness in his voice: "The Son of
man is come to seek and to save that which is lost";[8] and
where is the respectable, selfish, ambitious churchman
who is not made to wince as he hears the words to the
sons of Zebedee: "The Son of man came not to be
ministered unto, but to minister, and to give his life a
ransom for many?" [9]

What does one make of these words: "*I came*" . . .
"*I was sent*"? They have in them the passionate beat
of an urgent heart for all the downtrodden men and
women who walked the lanes and byways of his native

land. Where did he get this message? What was the genesis of this universe of life? The barren, mechanical explanation of the dogmatist that confidently affirms that everything Jesus said and did was the result of his conscious pre-existence makes a mockery of his gospel, and becomes an escape mechanism from reality. Nothing can be taken from Jesus that came to him by way of his spiritual kinship with his Father, but when one meets him along the pathway of his earthly experience, one knows him as a man in the world of men, and that his longing for a Divine-Human brotherhood lay along moral and psychological pathways, both in respect to whence it came and its significance to the generations that have followed his.

What took him away from the carpenter's bench in Nazareth into the solitariness of the wilderness? What kept him pounding the dusty roads, treading the streets of villages and crowded cities, and finally carrying a Cross up a hill called Calvary, only to be laid in the end in a borrowed grave which no man knows to this day? Somehow in this day when the intellectual and moral demands of men must be satisfied before we get a religion that is adequate to deal with the problems that confront a terrorized, harassed and frustrated world, the curious mind is not content with the traditional assumptions, their claim to finality, and their invocation to supernatural sanctions. But curiosity must be reverent, for no man can look into the heart of Jesus as he sought to reveal the human heart of God to men without recognizing that everywhere he walks,

> Earth's crammed with heaven,
> And every common bush afire with God;
> And only he who sees, takes off his shoes,
> The rest sit round it and pluck blackberries.[10]

The thing that strikes the observer as he sees Jesus stepping out upon the stage of the world's tragedy and woe is his consciousness of his own unbroken contact with God, and the dearth of religious vitality in the people around him. It was not easy to move out from a trade which promised at least physical security to himself and the family for which he was responsible. He left it only because there was nothing else his God-filled soul could do when he recognized the wistful appeal of a humanity starved in soul because of the absence of a God who could satisfy their deepest hunger.

For thirty years he had been engaged not only in making a living, but in examining his heart under the light of his Father's presence. There was a long interval between his visit to the Temple at the age of twelve and the day when he went out to join his cousin John at the Jordan. But when that period of discipline in the school of life had passed, and he had experienced one fresh discovery after the other, of God, he not only knew what his work should be, but looking out over the seething mass of humanity

> He took the suffering human race,
> He read each wound, each weakness clear;
> And struck his finger on the place,
> And said, "thou ailest here and here!" [11]

A word may be needed here on the practical nature of mysticism. A mystic is all too frequently regarded as a man who spends his time contemplating God, becoming only a spectator of the passing scene and making no contribution toward building a truer spiritual life in the individual and a better social order. That idea stems out of our Occidental culture where contemplation has seemed to be a waste of time. Even the preacher has been inoculated with this deadly virus until he has come to believe and act as though the world will be saved by his always doing something, going somewhere, and attending committee meetings. But if one knows the history of the progress of religion it would be discovered that mystics all down through the ages have not been spiritual drones; "they have been hundred-horse-power persons pouring into the world of time their unwonted additions of spiritual energy." [12] It is true that mysticism has often taken the form of the abnormal and the mysterious, and has flourished along the edge of the trance and psychic miracle. But true mysticism is something fundamental to the nature of the soul, and a native capacity for intercourse and communion with God.

This was the mysticism of Jesus, the kind which William James describes as the person who has "windows through which the mind looks out upon a more extensive and inclusive world." [13] Without this experience there would have been no discovery of God's purpose for the world of men. What he sought was a life task that was bound up as intimately with God's purpose in the world as his own soul was bound up in the soul of God. And not only did he need to be endowed with the capacity to see God and understand his purposes, but there was the necessity likewise for a moral enthusiasm that could lead him to champion a great cause and effect a reformation.

Now after two thousand years of reading the record of his life one cannot fail to see the moral build and caliber of the Man. Not only was he endowed with unclouded vision of God, but he was gripped with a zeal that moved mountains of error and darkness from the world. He not only took time to go by himself for the purpose of contemplating God, but he stands before the world as a prophet and revolutionary. He was no idle dreamer, but a hero; not a Man who dwelt in the loveliness of his vision, but a crusader on life's battleground. He cannot be judged by our conventional standards. In fact, he himself pronounces his judgment upon most of the things which have been called Christian, and if men listen to him they will know that much of what goes by the name of Christianity he calls quackery and sham. When a cloak of sanctity is put about our dead conventions his soul flames into white-hot passion of scathing denunciation. Any picture that does not portray him as something more than the "sweet Jesus" would not only be incomplete, but a falsification of his character.

It is not enough to say that Jesus had a deep interest in "humanity." Crowds did not arouse in him the abstract enthusiasm of the sociologist or the scientific social reformer. When the writer recites the incident of the crowd that followed Jesus into the desert, he tells us that there were five thousand men besides women and children; but when Jesus wanted to feed them he felt the hunger that gnawed at each one's stomach. He never counted heads. Faces were not mere statues in physiognomy; they were histories of human lives. Human interests and conditions made their appeal to him, interest awoke sympathy, sympathy deepened into compassion, and compassion led him to heal, forgive and cleanse.

66

> And some, with wondrous tenderness,
> To his lips he gently pressed,
> And fervent blessings breathed on them,
> And laid them in his breast.[14]

It was this that so arrested the attention of Matthew the taxgatherer that he took his pen one day, and with a thrill that overtopped his hatred for those who persecuted him, wrote down what one of his Jewish ancestors had said, "Himself took our infirmities, and bare our sicknesses." [15] Nothing less could describe the sympathy that identified itself with every suffering soul. His heart was as sensitive as an aeolian harp that throbbed and responded to every note of sorrow and need. Doubtless the most revealing word ever spoken about him was what was remembered as he went from city to city and village to village where he encountered scores and scores of hopeless and despairing humans: "But when he saw the multitudes, he was moved with *compassion* on them, because they fainted, and were scattered abroad, as sheep having no shepherd." [16]

Was it only an expression of the face, only a twitch of the mouth, only a tear that he may have flicked from his cheek, that brought this descriptive word from the pen of the biographer? It was more than that. If one has the least insight into the compassionate heart of Jesus, and realizes how deeply he had drunk at the fountain of inspiration furnished by the great prophets of the past, one can almost read the indignation that welled up within him as he beheld the crime of the ruling classes against the common man, when he recalled a heroic Micaiah who spoke out on the eve of a national disaster, and paid the price for his fearlessness.[17] Blind, aimless, helpless folk, their religion all awry, because their leaders had deceived them, and there was no one to show them their way to God. Multitudes! Multitudes! Multitudes!—fainting, scattered abroad, harassed, burdened with a hundred precepts, homeless—many of them—wandering in the fields, hiding in dens and caves, blind guides that cursed them, starvation that would leave their stinking bodies by the roadside—all of them crying for a shepherd that had the face of God, and who would pull them out of the thicket of disease and penury, loneliness and frustration, and set their feet on the highway which shall be a highway of real holiness where the "ransomed of the Lord shall return, and come to Zion with songs and everlasting joy upon their heads" . . . and where they shall "obtain joy and gladness, and sorrow and sighing shall flee away." [18] This was the pity of God in Jesus of Nazareth, a pity that bends over the world, and sees, not masses, but men.

Place alongside of this his wail over the city of Jerusalem after his lengthy tirade against the leaders who had brought the people to the place where nothing but doom stared them in the face: "O Jerusalem, Jerusalem, thou that killest the prophets, and stonest them which are sent unto thee, how often would I have gathered thy children together, even as a hen gathered her chickens under her wings, and ye would not!" [19] Was there ever intercession such as this? It sounds like the ancient record which told of God "hovering over the waters" [20] on the first morning of creation. It was a brooding, sheltering, mothering pity for a city whose glory had faded and whose future was shrouded in gloom. And while he spoke, he wept.

When a will that is aglow with righteous fervor and a heart that is warm with love for human beings meet in a soul that is lighted up with an experience in God, then the only thing one can do is to wait until some clear evidence is given as to the direction one's life shall take. It must have been so with Jesus. Although the silent years in Nazareth reveal nothing of the places to which he went, the sights he saw, the searchings of spirit he had, nor the times he prayed in his trysting places with God, one can be sure he was seeking light along the paths that were still dark. What he said in his private prayers is not known, except that subsequent events suggest that when he sat in the synagogue, or went about his carpentering, or sought the silences of the hills, his mind must have swept the world until it saw men as exiles, robbed of their heritage in a God who loved them rather than a God who was waiting to take revenge on the dumb terror of his people. Through all their sorrows, diseases, burdens and wearinesses Jesus saw the wistful face of God looking for some deliverer.

Sermons have been preached and books written on the necessity and efficacy of prayer, but seldom do we think or speak of a praying God. Yet, who can hear Jesus praying and note the emotional upheaval of his heart in his public prayer without finding in it the echo of the yearning heart of God? Always as Jesus bent his sensitive spirit to catch the cry of the least, the last and the lost, it became to him the cry of God in his longing for fellowship with men. William Vaughn Moody could never think of a completed humanity without God, nor of a completed God without men. To think of God as a Being standing in lonely greatness and majesty demanding the praise and obeisance of his subjects is hardly a picture of the God in whom Jesus wanted to find his truest and highest self, and whom he saw as fashioning a body out of the wants and needs of the world of men.

> Then suddenly in my own heart
> I felt God walk and gaze about;
> He spoke; his words seemed held apart
> With gladness and with doubt.

"Here is my meat and wine," he said,
"My love, my toil, my ancient care;
Here is my cloak, my book, my bed,
And here my old despair;

"Here are my seasons: winter, and spring,
Summer the same, and autumn spills
The fruits I look for; everything
As on my heavenly hills." [21]

Those indescribable words which Jesus used at the close of his discourse just before they led him away to the court of Annas and Caiaphas: "Inasmuch as ye did it unto one of the least of these my brethren, ye have done it unto me," [22] ought to make us stop in our tracks and listen to the heartache of mankind as we hear the agonizing cry of God: I am hungry, feed me; thirsty, give me to drink; a stranger, shelter me; sick, and in prison, do come and sit by my bed. It is the prayer of God, the passion and pity of God praying to have the broken heart of mankind healed by some deed of love.

Millions on millions pray to me
Yet hearken not to hear me pray;
Nor comes there any to set me free
Of all who plead from night to day.
So God is mute and Heaven is still
While the nations kill.[23]

It is doing no violence to the character of Jesus to say that one day after years of searching his own heart, and trying to discover the path he should take, he looked up into the face of his Father and saw in it the sadness of human woe, and felt in that saddened countenance he was being confronted with the challenge to dedicate himself to the dire needs of the people. It was an experience similar to that of Paul when he confessed that he did not always know the form his prayer should take, but that "the Spirit itself maketh intercession for us with groanings which cannot be uttered." [24] Jesus at prayer was God at prayer, and the fountain of living water which took its source in the heart of God became in him what he told the Woman of Samaria, "a spring of water welling up to life eternal." [25] Jesus became the outgoing of the divine will in service, and as one watches his movements and hears his voice, the heart instinctively says,

> Our restless spirits yearn for Thee,
> Where'er our changeful lot is cast,
> Glad when Thy gracious smile we see,
> Blest when our faith can hold Thee fast.[26]

Jesus, however, did not become the express image of God, and find his will blending perfectly with the will of his Father, only because his days were steeped in prayer. While it is certain that no man can find the

God of Jesus without praying as he prayed, it is also true that God is of little value to the man who is unaware of the condition of the social environment around him. One cannot think of Jesus' acceptance of the approval of God at the Jordan, "This is my beloved Son, in whom I am well pleased," without feeling that those years in Nazareth at the carpenter's bench, in the streets and homes, found him looking with eyes of sympathy and love upon the heartaches of his people. "Though I speak with the tongues of men and of angels, and have not love, I am become as sounding brass, or a tinkling cymbal," said Paul long after Jesus said, "Thou shalt love the Lord thy God . . . and thy neighbor as thyself." What Paul found wrong with the world was the same as Jesus had found: a lack of fellowship. Man finds his true life in the life of his fellows, and men find their way to fellowship and true human intercourse when they have won their way out into the light of God's presence. The measure of a man's distance from his fellows is the measure of his distance from God.

The first thing Jesus saw which told him how far man had wandered from the original intent of God was the distance that one class had put between itself and another class. The thing that made the religion of his day a mere ritual was this barrier which not only separated class from class, but separated both from God. This knowledge did not come to him after he embarked upon his ministry. What he said about it in parables was reminiscent of what he had seen for thirty years. Dives, for instance, must have been a familiar figure in Nazareth, and the nearby places he had visited; Dives clothed in purple and fine linen and the compassion that may have once been his now well-nigh extinguished, and Lazarus, lying at his gate, his foul rags pleading for a bit of kindness and finding it only in the tongues of the parish dogs. There is little capacity for the reception of divine mercy in a man whose springs of pity and compassion have dried up, and the fixed gulf across which Dives looked upon Lazarus is only eternity's counterpart of the social cleft which Dives himself had insisted on making. Or, as in the case of the Rich Fool, when death takes from him the "much goods" in which his soul was engrossed, it takes his soul's life also. "What shall I do, because I have not where to bestow my fruits?" could well have found an answer in the sickness to heal and the nakedness to clothe in the community.

Only a man bereft of God and absolutely self-centered would propose to spend the rest of his days on the pleasures of his body. The tragedy is, that not only do Dives and the Rich Fool lose their souls, but in their attitude toward human misery the oppressed become envious, and envy is a co-partner of covetousness. How to overcome selfish indifference on the part of the people with "much goods," and the bitter enmity of the oppressed, was the social problem that Jesus found. It is our problem, too.

There was, however, one class of mammon worshiper that attracted Jesus and quickened his sympathy. It was the taxgatherer who had become a social and political outcast. Many a publican such as Zacchaeus had become mired in the sticky clay of avarice largely because of the sanctimonious prayer of the Pharisee with its note of superior disdain: "God, I thank thee that I am not as other men, . . . or even as this publican," which he had heard on many occasions. He had given up going to the synagogue and accepted his place in society as a black sheep. Day by day he had grown harder by reason of the place to which he had been assigned by the standards of society. One can hear the laughter of himself with his fellow publicans, a laughter that was only a cover-up for the friendship he craved. The crowd on the streets of Jericho which had elbowed him into a tree was a symbol to Jesus of the barrier of social ostracism which he had seen in the town of Nazareth, and which spelled separation from God both for the publican and for those who stood against him.

The boon companion of the publican was the harlot. Strange as it may seem, the pride of lust is never so hard to pierce as is the pride of avarice. Jesus found it so and the record of the Gospels is evidence that he got the readiest response from the slaves of passion and lust. Nevertheless, one stands appalled before the sight of a human personality becoming degraded to the point of where sensual gratification becomes the end-all and be-all of life. The soul gets lost like a sheep wandering in a lonely wilderness, like a piece of money which has rolled away into a dark corner, no longer of any value; or like a lad with all the rich treasures of the human heart becoming befouled and wasted in a morass of riotous living in a far country. All this, no doubt, Jesus had seen long before he left the village of Nazareth.

But deeper than all the tragedy of lostness described by Jesus in three matchless parables lies the picture of God which they draw. It is God who feels the loss, and in the words, "While he was yet a great way off his father saw him," one gets a profoundly moving glimpse of the great, yearning, broken heart of God. And because Jesus felt the same strong emotion as did God at the sight of the wretchedness of men, he was constrained to say, "I am sent to seek and to save the lost." As the tide of human wretchedness swept by his door every day during his years in Nazareth, every painful story that met his eyes went into the building of a heart that would lay itself under the woes and miseries of men.

The highest barrier of all, however, which he saw reared between people and God, was the barrier of rabbinnical tradition, priestly ritual and ceremony. The priest, the scribe and the Pharisee had locked the gates of the Kingdom so tightly that they themselves could not enter, nor would they suffer others to do so. Their tithes of mint, anise and cummin, their meticulous peddling of precept, the unreality of their external forms of religion, their disdaining of people who did not know the Law, and their seeking after God everywhere except in the sanctuary of the heart became the disruptive element in society, and separated both the priest and the people from God. As Jesus looked upon this state of affairs in the religious life of his people his heart longed for a leader and shepherd who could giude them back to God. When he saw the restlessness of the people because one hope after another flickered out, he discovered that what was once a longing for spiritual things had now become a base and earthly hope for a political leader who could save them from a corrupt political oppression. But in any true reading of the experience of Jesus we shall have to conclude that any Messianic hope about which he had read in the prophetic writings of those who had gone before him, spoke a language to his soul other than that which bred a fanatical zeal in his breast for the restoration of Israel's glorious past. He believed that the realization of the will of his father would have to come in human life. It was a moral and spiritual reformation which should have to be the desire of his people.

No better proof that this was to be the course of his ministry can be found than that which constituted the theme of his opening campaign: "The kingdom of God is at hand." It was not a Messiah who had come, but a Kingdom. One by one he saw the empires of his day catching the vision of the Son of Man and becoming kingdoms of humanity where power was no longer to be that of brute force, but a power which was born in the love-heart of God. This was the vision that seized, and shook, and molded the Nazareth Carpenter's soul, a Divine-Human Brotherhood which should rise above the misery and restlessness, the tangle and discord of his day.

It sounds like a vain and unreal hope, especially in view of the fact that nations are living in the grip of fear and suspicion toward each other. Even so, the hope still holds, for it has ever been the prophecy of all the great ones of earth. It is the ultimate goal toward which God moves in nature and human history. All the great philosophers and all the great shining lights from Plato to Kant and to men of our own day tell us of their hope for universal peace where nations shall live together in co-operation and brotherhood. It is More's *Utopia*, a Kingdom of Humanity, the New Atlantis, the Parliament of Man, the League of Nations, the United Nations. It is Augustine's City of God, the Kingdom of Heaven. To be sure, there are imperfections, and the

good purposes of God often come to naught, and the
world is tottering now on the brink of another disaster.
A post-hydrogen-bomb civilization is horrible to contem-
plate. But men are telling us that we are inevitably
moving in that direction. Still men who stake their faith
in God will go on believing in a Divine-Human Brotherhood because it represents the deepest longing of the
human heart. Such longing cannot be forever denied.
Someday it will find its fulfillment in the prophetic
utterance of the noblest and holiest reformer of them
all—Jesus of Nazareth.

There was nothing provincial or nationalistic about
the Kingdom of which he spoke. He saw the wide-
range view of the missionary Jonah. He looked for the
doing of God's will not only in Palestine, but on the
earth: "Thy will be done on earth as it is in heaven."
When he chose followers he told them they were to be
salt, not of Israel, but of the earth, and the light, not
only of Galilee, but of the world. And sometimes as he
looked he saw men coming from the East and the West,
the North and the South, to sit down in the Kingdom
of his Father.

Men have talked of the originality of Jesus as though
what he said had never been thought or spoken of before. But he would be the last to lay claim to any such
distinction. He was bringing things new and old out of
the treasure house of the past, and the manner of his

making all things new was to fulfill the best and the noblest of the past. He lopped off the dead accretions and made what was true and real stand out in glorious splendor. He scotched the superstitions of the day, stripped his message of all localism and nationalism, and saw the day when the earth should be full of the knowledge of the Lord as the waters cover the sea. This was the highest desire of God for mankind, and there was no price too great for Jesus to pay for its realization. It would be not so much a human achievement as a gift of God, and was reserved for those whose hearts would be as little children's hearts, and who would open their lives to receive him.

This was reality to Jesus. He heard it knocking at the door of human life. It had eternity in it, and someday it would be realized. When that time should come the false principle of self-assertion, blind pride, brute force, and intelligent national self-interest which seems to be the basis upon which we hope to set the world's house in order will go. The Kingdom can be nothing less than a Kingdom of love, and the source of human brotherhood found in the desire of men to learn how to become sons of God.

Men have called him a fanatic and have said that much of his teaching was colored by the apocalyptic fancies of his day. And surely no one would be so rash as to declare Jesus was not a child of his age and that he was not steeped in the current thought. But when one fastens the term "fanatic" on him, implying that he was intoxicated with a mad dream, out of touch with all the clamor and emptiness of human life, and that in in the end he flung his life away for a dream in the clouds, one must ask oneself, How could a man with such hallucinations still live?

May it not be that we shall yet have to go back to him to learn how far we have gone astray; to discover how far we have lost touch with a reality he grasped?

IV

The Urge that Drove Him to His Task

---

*I*T WAS to the spirit of a mature man long steeped in wonderings about the world's far drift from God, to a man conscious of the presence of God in his own life and of an urgent desire for a society where God should reign, to a spirit that had wrestled the night through on the hills of Nazareth, that the news came stealing into the workshop of a movement that had begun and was gaining momentum along the banks of the Jordan. One can imagine the look in the eyes of this humble toiler as he laid down his tools, leaned his back against the bench, and listened as one neighbor after another brought the report of how John was calling the people to repentance. The hands on his clock of destiny were moving slowly but surely; one day the hour would strike when he, too, would move out upon the broad field of adventure.

The stories drifted in of the crowds that were flocking down to the river, of how one band of pilgrims after another from all the region round about were on their way to listen to this rugged man with eyes aflame and whose one message was "Repent." The slumbering conscience of Israel was awake; the hand was knocking at the nation's heart, putting complacency to flight, and bringing a quivering, terrified people face to face with moral and religious failure. "Lord, how long shall the wicked triumph?" [1] was the sigh of many a pious Israelite.

But here in the faces of the sweeping multitude on the way to repentance was written the promise of a speedy deliverance. Where John was baptizing and issuing his clarion call to the endless procession of penitents, they remembered the story of how Elijah had parted the waters with his mantle and was taken up into heaven in a chariot of fire. Many a Passover night they had left the door of their home open, hoping he would return. Doubtless now they stood with their faces toward the sky hoping for his return as he had departed on the clouds of heaven. Still John cried, "Make straight the way of the Lord." Only by universal repentance could a condition be created suitable for the Messiah's appearance. Such was the apocalyptic hope of Israel.

Something more significant than this, however, was stirring in the breast of Jesus as he listened to the tales told in Nazareth by the returning pilgrims. To him, God was making a fresh entrance into the life of his native land. Much as he differed later from John, he never doubted the quality of John's life. John seemed to epitomize every good thing that men had labored and struggled for through all the past centuries of sorrow and blunder. It was this movement inaugurated by John that marked the turning point in the world's religious history. Prophets had dreamed and spoken about it, but never did it become a reality until John stood on the banks of the Jordan and declared that "every valley shall be filled, and every mountain and hill shall be brought low; and the crooked shall be made straight, and the rough ways shall be made smooth." [2] The Kingdom of God was at hand and men were violently breaking into it. At last, at last, Jesus felt his day had come.

No doubt the family of Jesus would go down to the Jordan. But not now. The movement had been on foot for some time before Jesus appeared on the scene. One wonders why. His reluctance to rush off at once was not due to his hesitancy to abandon his work as a carpenter, or to renounce the secular task for that of an itinerant preacher. His commitment to God and his trust in God's care for him had been made long before. The idea of a Kingdom of righteousness was not new to him. His dictum, "Seek ye first the kingdom of God, and his righteousness; and all these things shall be added unto you," was not uttered on the spur of the moment. It came out of the depth of his experience through the

Nazareth years, and to lay down his tools at once and join John in his religious movement would have been as easy as stepping across the threshold of his home into the morning's sunshine.

Nor did his home ties have anything to do with his hesitancy. There is ample evidence in the Gospels that the severance of these bonds was no easier for him than for any other devoted son and brother in Israel. "Foxes have holes, and birds of the air have nests; but the Son of man hath not where to lay his head" [3] was the cry of a homesick soul for a bed and a meal in the cottage of Nazareth. But long before John appeared at the Jordan the instincts of his soul told him that one day his life's toil would be devoted, not merely to the little family in Nazareth, but to the family of God. There never was a day at home when he was not willing to follow the clear direction of the Father's will.

No, the cause of the hesitancy ran deeper. John's call was a call to Repentance. It was a charge against the dark sins of the people. The report of what was happening at the Jordan is sketchy, but in imagination one sees multitudes hastening there in search of something that would cure the inner unrest, the want, and the discord of life. What shall we do then? was on the lips of every pilgrim, the publican, the Pharisee and the soldier. John truckled to no man. One thing he demanded from all was repentance, and before he would baptize, they must first cleanse themselves in their own purifying tears.

But in the God-filled soul of Jesus there was no longing for something not yet attained. This uninterrupted communion of the soul of Jesus with God was coming into conflict with the motives that were driving people to John's baptism. There never was a time in his life when he felt the need of a spiritual rebirth. His was a once-born life. He drank in God's spirit with his mother's milk, learned God's father-love from Joseph, and heard the voice of the divine approval at the age of twelve in the Temple. Nothing finer could have been said about him than that he "increased in wisdom and stature, and in favour with God and men."

There is nothing here that smacks of self-righteousness. It is rather a chastity of soul, an inner impulse to guard the precious gifts of God bestowed upon him every time he opened his soul to the gracious influence of his Father's love. In it there was no arrogance, no denunciation of John, no desire to set John aside, no feeling that a rival had arisen to challenge his own sense of place and power in building a Kingdom of righteousness. Many big men of history set out to break their rivals; but not so Jesus. On the contrary, John's movement caught his ear, and somehow in the depth of his own soul he must have heard the rising, swelling beat of humanity's misery, and recognized that he too would

have to launch his bark on that swelling sea. Who knows
but in that hour he may have sensed the agony of soul it
would require to bear a beaten humanity back to God
and show it God's love in a sacrificial life and death?

Once convinced that John's message had in it the
revelation of God, he arose, bade his mother and brethren farewell, walked out of Nazareth "one summer
morning along the dusty ways and through the scrubby
hills, making for the pools of Jordan. He joined the
throng of troubled seekers whose anxious feet had beaten
paths like sheep-tracks through the rough country. He
mingled humbly with this pilgrim mob until they
brought him to the motley concourse at the river. There
he stayed all day, watching with loving eyes this great
sacrament of the people's awakening and cleansing.
Then, as twilight gathered and the weary people trudged
homewards—some, praise God, with lighter hearts—
Jesus, 'when all the people were baptized,' went up to
John." [4]

One wonders how long he talked with John, and what
they said to each other. We have a few words: "I have
need to be baptized of thee, and comest thou to me? . . .
Suffer it to be so now: for thus it becometh us to fulfill
all righteousness." [5] Cousins though they were there is
no evidence that they had ever seen or known each
other. Indeed, if one relies on the record of John's Gospel when Jesus came to the Jordan he was not recog-

nized by John. So they must have gone apart and talked with each other, and Jesus would commend John on the boldness of his utterances, on his prophetic vision, how he stood in the long succession of Israel's prophets, and how he was thrilled when he heard back in Nazareth of the movement toward the rebirth of the nation. He might have told John of his own boyhood days, of what he had seen as a lad of the insurrectionist movement in Sepphoris, of his visit to the Temple, and of the thoughts he had as he worked and toiled for a living in Nazareth. Likely he did not forget to tell John of the influence of his father and mother on his own life, and how he had long since committed himself to the will of his heavenly Father and how he was waiting and praying for the day when he could join a movement which would set his country free, not by an army, but by taking into its life the spirit which had been born in his own soul. The deliverer he conceived of was somewhat different from the one John envisioned. He would have no fan in his hand, no fire to consume his enemies. Only the purging power of love could supplant the hatred and revenge in men's hearts.

He must have convinced John of his own purity of mind and heart, of his desire to link himself with the best that men had struggled for down through the ages, that he too had the instincts of a prophet, and that the desire of the ages could be fulfilled in men who

were born in the spirit of God. He would tell John that
he could not hold himself aloof from a movement which
promised so much, and that here he was stepping on the
threshold of the Kingdom of God around which all his
holiest longings gathered. He must give himself to it as
a humble laborer. He would submit to John's baptism.
He had no confession to make. His baptism did not
signify that he had renounced one principle or law of
life and adopted another. What he wanted to do was
to take an open vow of sacramental self-dedication.
Body, soul and spirit would be dedicated in service to
his fellows. He would lay himself alongside their misery,
bear their infirmities, and show them their way back
to God. This was the righteousness it became him to
fulfill.

Perhaps never before the hour of baptism did it come
to him that God's full purpose should be fulfilled in him,
that the suffering servant of Yahweh Isaiah spoke of
should be gathered up in a single representative personality, the Son of Man. Having lived in intimate relationship with his Father during all of the Nazareth years,
and humbly obedient to every fresh glimpse of the
Father's will, here at the Jordan he was confronted with
his own significance, the part he would have to play
toward the realization of the Kingdom, the vision of
which had gripped his young mind and heart. As Holtzmann has so well said, "Jesus' baptismal experience is

thus the vision of his call, is analogous to the visions which the Old Testament prophets had at their respective calls. It may also be compared to the conversion of Paul, which was equivalent to a call to be the great apostle to the Gentiles. In all these cases the visionary perception is accompanied by a visionary hearing of a voice, and in each case alike the consequence for the person who has the vision is a complete transformation of his life." [6]

"Why don't voices come to me?" asked Charles of St. Joan. "I'm king, you are not."

"They do come to you," replied Joan, "but you do not hear them. You have not sat in the field in the evening listening for them. When the angelus rings you cross yourself and have done with it; but if you prayed from your heart, and listened to the thrilling of the bells in the air after they stop ringing, you would hear the voice as well as I do." [7]

Jesus had sat in the fields long hours listening for the voice of God; now at the Jordan the heavens opened over his soul, and he heard in clear accents the voice of God sealing the transaction: "Thou art my beloved Son, in thee I am well pleased." Where had he heard that word "Son" before but in the second Psalm? Perhaps he had recalled it that day as a child in the Temple: "Thou art my Son; this day have I begotten thee." [8] And the words, "in thee I am well pleased," were the echo of the other words, "mine elect, in whom my soul delight-eth." [9] What a glorious blending of the consciousness of being Son with the consciousness that he was not Lord and Master but a servant! Without finding God he could find no commitment to a life's task.

Here was the urge that drove him to his task. Here was the awakening to a divine commission. "Even in the soberest conception of human history this moment is one of the greatest turning-points in the world's de-velopment." [10] History has always turned around great personalities, and in the greatness of personalities the age moves on to greater perfection. "When the Master of the universe has points to carry in his government he impresses his will in the structure of minds." [11]

He could not go back to Nazareth now. Nor could he live day by day in ecstasy. He had to think over this Jordan experience, to be as utterly alone as a man could be. "Then was Jesus led up of the Spirit into the wilderness to be tempted of the devil." The lonely and desolate region lying beyond the river offered the ideal place where he could indulge his soul in wrestling and conflict. But to describe a dialogue between Jesus and a plain and obvious devil, with horned hoofs and spear-point tail, would be to make a mockery of this wilderness vigil. Through that haunted and sinister atmosphere instead there came and stood out before him in bold relief, confronting his soul, the Spirit of the World.

There in that region of black land, spined with shrubs, a place of deathlike silence, broken only by the cry of vultures sailing overhead, he faced the new situation which his baptism had created and which his acceptance of divine vocation had forced upon him.

It was not a conflict of doubt concerning the discovery of himself, but a conflict of doubt as to the way he should take. The problem of evil which has always perplexed the mind of man never gave him the slightest concern. He knew that God meant to triumph, and that all the ugliness of evil represented by the devil would pass away as a hideous dream just as soon as the world's heart could understand the awakening touch of love. It was the struggle of ultimate and final choice between two opposing ways of fulfilling his divine task.

That such a struggle could go on in the soul of a Man who had already surrendered himself and come to the place of self-dedication to a particular work is not only psychologically possible, but is amply demonstrated in the experiences of Jesus. When he says in response to his Mother's plea that he go back home with them, "Whosoever shall do the will of God, the same is my brother, and my sister, and my mother," or when he not only prays, "Thy kingdom come," but "Thy will be done," or when at the last his own shuddering body knelt in the garden and out of the agony of his heart he prayed, "Not my will but thine be done," we sense a reverberation of the struggle in the wilderness, and recognize them as so many signals thrown up out of the deeps of his utter self-identification with the will of God.

More than that, the struggle in the wilderness was not a question as to whether he should be obedient or disobedient, but a question as to whether the way he should take would be the way that God wanted him to take. A man gets further in his understanding of the temptation story if he sees in it a human Jesus struggling to understand the mind and will of God. Moreover, though the victory was complete in the wilderness, there was yet the necessity right down to the end on the Cross, of a continual process of offering up his will to God. "Let him that thinketh he standeth take heed lest he fall," [12] was a mandate as true for Jesus as it is for us.

When one looks at the three temptations, one sees in them the suggestions of material magic, dazzling wonder and political achievement. What else were they but the apocalyptic dreams with which he was surrounded and with which the religious atmosphere of that day was charged? Each response of Jesus was taken from the old Deuteronomic law: "Man shall not live by bread alone," "Thou shalt not tempt the Lord thy God," and "Thou shalt worship the Lord thy God, and him only shalt thou serve." [13] These were the early lessons Jesus had learned; they constituted his boyhood morning and evening prayers, and in the use of them here his soul was fighting its way back from the polluted stream of religion in which his people were immersed, to the clear and cleansing spring which had been the source from which their morals and religion had taken their rise. If he walked the earth today he would again be engaged in a struggle to release his people from the follies and superstitions which have retarded the progress of the Kingdom of God as the result of the dogmas woven about his person. Today as then he would like to become God's lowly messenger to the deepest needs of the human heart.

Men so frequently have dulled their ears. But if they draw near with a reverent heart and a sensitive soul as they remember their own struggles in the hour of crisis, they catch something of what it meant to Jesus, conscious as he was of a unique sonship with God, as he wrestles inwardly in a solitary place with the temptation to compromise his own principles, to listen to the Spirit of the World.

"Son of God!" He heard those words at the Jordan and believed them. Now he hears them again. "If thou be the Son of God, command that these stones be made bread." What measureless power was his! Not for himself, but for the world that so needed God. He was hungry and the world was hungry. He could feed himself and the world, because power had been put into his hands. *Make these stones bread!*" He saw humanity stretching out before him like an endless sea: mothers clasping puny children to their dry and shriveled breasts, fathers with bony arms and legs, despair looking out of their eyes, all pleading for bread to eat. Hunger was the supreme problem of life; how was he to meet it? Surely to bring the Kingdom of God to such a world as this was first to banish every kind of want. He saw the upturned faces of men and women and children as in a waking dream. What could be stronger proof of the divine authority in him than to stay their bodily hunger? Let him make stones into bread!

From boyhood he had been familiar with the hope of Israel's leaders. Whenever men spoke of Israel's hope and destiny, this subject of bread was uppermost in their minds. An age of plenty—what was that but an echo of the prophetic phrase about the ploughman overtaking the reaper, the hills melting, and the mountains dropping sweet wine? Bone of his ancestors' bone and flesh of their flesh, he felt with them until compassion had become the mainspring of his life. He had seen beggars outside his carpenter shop in Nazareth. He had seen bitter disappointment, and looked upon poverty-stricken men and women moving with unshod and bruised feet over miles and miles of dirty streets. Deep within him and high above him, voices called to make the fight in behalf of his people for bread.

It is not necessary to argue the right of man to be

95

properly clothed and fed. Common-sense men have long since learned that Communism feeds and spreads upon poverty. The crying shame of our day is that there is bread enough and to spare, and yet people go hungry. There is no need to contend that people have the right to be healthy. The entire medical world is committed toward keeping people physically strong and to lengthen the span of life. Our age has long since ceased to regard poverty as a virtue. On the other hand, it may well be aware of what happens to a man or a nation when no heed is paid to bodily discipline. The legendary figure of Don Juan stalks through the pages of literature as a warning to those whose chief interest in life is physical enjoyment. You know the story: after killing a man he placed his statue at the top of the tomb. Later, inside the tomb, he gave a banquet to his friends, dragged the statue down from its place, and set it alongside him at the table. During the course of the banquet the marble statue arose, took Don Juan by the neck, and dragged him down to hell.

Living by bodily appetite is inviting death to dine with us. The boredom, the moodiness, the weariness and loneliness of life, written upon the faces of the devotees of the table, are only the evidences that the soul has begun to die. When men are concerned only with what they shall eat, and wherewithal they shall be clothed, they are creating Don Juan's marble statue.

To listen to the world's carnal clamor, and to found a Kingdom by appeals to bodily gratification, would have made him only a Bread-Messiah, not a physician of souls. To make bread cheap by miracle would not change the world into the Kingdom of God. There would be bread enough and to spare in the Kingdom, but it would be because love ruled and love shared. To admit that kinship with God is proved by satisfying the demand for bread at no cost is to admit that bread-making is the essential function of God. "I have meat to eat that ye know not of," he said to the disciples at Jacob's well. "My meat is to do the will of him that sent me." [14]

Here in the wilderness he had settled the problem that if ever the time should come when God's word in him should lead him to the place where danger threatened his physical existence, still he would have to obey God. All through his Nazareth life he had fed his soul on the first principles of true religion: "He humbled thee, and suffered thee to hunger, and fed thee with manna, which thou knewest not, neither did thy fathers know; that he might make thee know that man doth not live by bread alone, but by every word that proceedeth out of the mouth of the Lord doth man live." [15] He was waiting for a word that would make its response to the hunger of the soul, not to the hunger of men's bodies. True life would be found when God's spirit passed through the soul of Jesus, and thus passed from heart to heart.

A second time the Master soliloquizes as the Spirit of the World speaks again. It is a demonic voice, "yet all in the garb and tones of sanctity this time, speaking the very language of Holy Writ. . . . The vision changes, and the rock on which he sits on the steep hillsides shapes itself on his fancy as the Temple's cornerstone." [16] "Show us a sign," clamor the priest, the scribe, the Pharisee, the religious bigot, the arrogant authority. "If thou be the Son of God, cast thyself down: for it is written, He shall give his angels charge concerning thee: and in their hands they shall bear thee up, lest at any time thou dash thy foot against a stone."

It was the Ego speaking: Startle the world! Silence the priest and scribe by some spectacular act! This subtle temptation carried in it the germ of death to the spirit of self-effacement, unobtrusive gentleness, sympathy, love and humility which constitute the only means by which the Kingdom can be planted in men's hearts. This was the temptation to build a world on superstition rather than on true religion. The soul has a strange way of presuming on the laws of spiritual power entrusted to it. But down through the ages God has ever tried to make men love him, not fear him; to hate evil, not dread the punishment of evil; to make men love the good, not the reward of being good. "Thou shalt not tempt the Lord

thy God" by appealing to him for what we can get out
of it, for immunity from disaster because we are good,
by making promises to God so long as we enjoy material
welfare. Let us thank God for Jesus who refused the
legions of angels all the way from the wilderness to
Pilate's judgment hall, and who chose God for his own
eternal worth alone.

It is not too difficult for us to understand the successful resistance to the first two temptations which had to
do with base material cravings and the perversion of the
deepest instinct of the soul. But it is not so easy to understand how Jesus could refuse a throne. "All these things
will I give thee, if thou wilt fall down and worship me."
Did Edmund Burke not have it right in his speech on
Conciliation: "All government,—indeed, every human
benefit and enjoyment, every virtue and every prudent
act—is founded on compromise and barter"? Long
before the time of Jesus, Plato had been lured by the
idea of a perfect state where the philosopher, the sage,
the real aristocrat would be king. It would have been so
much easier for Jesus to play up to the ruling class in
order to restore the throne of David and make the
prophets' dream come true. By steady strides Jesus could
climb to the world's throne by the world's ways.

For a man to say that he is never a compromiser
marks him as an idiot. He is a compromiser by the mere
fact of his living in the world where his own well-being

sometimes stems out of the cruel and dishonest practices of men about him. He is caught in a web of evil to which he himself may have wittingly or unwittingly contributed, and he has the choice either of giving his own unqualified witness to the good life by lighting his candle on the altar of God's love and mercy, and thus helping to light candles all round the world, or commit suicide. But such compromise is quite different from the deliberate compromises made in the interest of self. Mephistopheles meets the old man Faust, and promises him youth and success if only he will sign the agreement. This he does, but in his desire to possess the world he loses his soul. Is that only a play on the stage? Far from that, the drama is a daily experience. There are a thousand forms in which one may be asked if one desires a trifling acknowledgment, a mere recognition—the kingdoms of the world. One may get them, but one cannot make up one's mind to have them without entailing the loss of one's own unique and priceless soul.

"Fall down and worship me." Alexander did it; so did Napoleon, the Hitlers and the Mussolinis. They said a nation can grow only from military might. We have never quite said that. We have said that it is spiritual quality that counts, and that the force we use is not for comfort, but for our own security and the welfare and the peace of the world. But the question must always arise in the honest man's heart, Can you conquer by force, even for God, without loss of purity, without falling down and worshiping the devil?

Jesus was perfectly willing to die, but not for a crumbling kingdom such as was dangled before his ambitions. Every nation built on any other foundation than that of love and helpfulness carries within itself the germs of its own decay. Jesus wanted something that would last, a community of souls loyal to truth, faithful to the good, and dedicated to love and justice, where men could find an ever-deepening satisfaction for their strongest and most imperative desires. There was to be no short-cut of forceful self-assertion, no self-appointed benefactor; but the way of self-surrender to the democracy of God, the way of self-effacement and sacrifice. "Thou shalt worship the Lord thy God, and him only shalt thou serve." Nothing can be made out of Jesus' reply than this: I'd like to see what the heavenly power of love flowing through me can do. If that means sacrifice and sorrow, let me still do it. I must take God's way, not yours. Power he wanted. Otherwise his life would be futile. But power could not be debased and centered about selfish desires. It had to be achieved in the light of heaven's demands, the demands of self-surrender and sacrifice. He emerged from the temptations as Lord of himself, at peace and rest in his soul.

With sure and certain step he left the wilderness, and turned, not in the direction of Nazareth, but to Capernaum. He knew the way he must take, what the nature and essence of his task should be. Now the people who sat in darkness would see a great light, and the shadow and death with which they were surrounded should spring into light. Now the burden of his message would be, "The time is fulfilled, and the kingdom of God is at hand: repent ye, and believe the gospel." [17] He was the herald of the Kingdom and the revealer of the will of God. What he would say, how he would act, and what would be the nature of his work, were not born out of his own initiative, but the result of the all-constraining will of Another—God. "Thy will be done," "This is the Father's will which sent me," was the source of his purpose in life. All the passion, all the trust, all the confidence of a God-sent life were his, just as Jeremiah before him had found: "His word was in mine heart as a burning fire shut up in my bones, and I was weary with forbearing, and could not stay," and of Paul behind him, "Necessity is laid upon me; yea, woe is unto me, if I preach not the gospel!" [18] The dead past was forgotten and cast away, but the living past with its ageless truth furnished the authority with which he would speak, and the urgent and honest proclamation of his message arose out of the desperate bodily and spiritual conditions around him.

Before long angry cries were being raised against him. What seemed sacred to the pious was being destroyed.

The countless practices which had been laid upon the backs of the people whereby they should gain favor with God he was roundly denouncing. But Jesus protested this charge of irreverence for the past. "Think not that I am come to destroy the law, or the prophets: I came not to destroy, but to fulfil." A lifelong study of the law and the prophets had given him a holy reverence for the past. He was not a breaker of the teachings of his fathers, but a builder upon the foundation of truth and righteousness. What he saw was the quenching of the spirit in his day which had been the quickening breath of his fathers who had brought the law and the prophets to life. He saw the mountain of rabinnical tradition, priestly ritual and ceremony, which had throttled the spirit of God in the lives of the people. He wanted to gather up again all the moral and religious principles which had once been the possession of the saints in Israel's history. He had come to replace the cold externality of the law which had been thrust upon the people, with an inward sanctity and a living soul. In fact, he was calling the people back to the heart of religion, to justice, mercy and faith; to what had echoed and re-echoed in the prophetic writings—mercy instead of sacrifice, to do justly, love mercy, and walk humbly before God. Only this could fit them for fellowship with God and give them citizenship in the Kingdom.

When one reads the parable of the Rich Fool one dis-

covers in him the supreme egotist. In the brief mono-
logue of sixty-one words, the word "I" occurs six times
and "my" or "mine" six times, and in doing so he earned
the title of "Thou Fool!" Jesus too used the word "I"
on numerous occasions, but in the use of it there is no
repellent egotism. When he said "I tell you" six times in
the fifth chapter of Matthew the pronoun served no
purpose of exalting himself. He said it because he was
lost to himself and dedicated to an urgent and com-
manding cause. He was the servant of the Kingdom and
when he said to the emissaries of the wavering and discouraged John in prison, "What went ye out for to see?
A prophet? Yea, *I tell you*, more than a prophet," and
when he stood up in the synagogue of Nazareth and said
"The Spirit of the Lord is upon *me* . . . he sent me.
. . . This day this Scripture is fulfilled in your hearing," it was because he felt that God's mantle had been
thrown about his shoulders, that he had been invested
with divine authority to preach the Gospel to the poor,
bring release to the captives, recovery of sight to the
blind, free the oppressed, and proclaim the year of the
Lord's favor.

It was the world's need that concerned him, that
quickened his pulse beat, and that made his life throb
and glow with a consecrated passion. When the crowds
pressed upon him, and the demons cried in his ears, so
that the nights became sleepless for him, and he stole

through the streets before dawn to a place where he
could rest his weary soul and pray, and then move on to
the country towns, one catches the pathos of the deep
emotion that surged in his being because of the sense
of responsibility. And as he walked along and beheld
the reapers putting the sickle into the ripened grain he
saw the world as a great harvest field waiting to be
gathered into barns before it should fall of its own weight
and the precious grains be lost to the farmer. "The harvest is rich, but the laborers are few; so pray the Lord
of the harvest to send laborers to gather his harvest." [19]
The world was the harvest and he was the reaper. So
much to do and so little time! One single soul, one body,
one pair of hands! God, send more reapers into the
harvest field!

After awhile the Cross loomed in his pathway. There
were evidences all along the way that a Man of his sort
could not long survive the prejudices of an embittered
aristocracy. "I will send them prophets and apostles,
some they will kill and some they will persecute; it was
that the blood of all the prophets shed from the foundation of the world might be charged upon this generation,
from the blood of Abel down to the blood of Zachariah
who was slain between the altar and the House of God
—yes, I tell you, it will be charged upon this generation." [20] Cruel death at the hands of enemies was in the
offing. "I have a baptism to undergo—what tension I

suffer, till it is all over!" [21] But that would not be the end. The cry of victory was heard beneath the passionate outbursts, and one feels as one reads the confidence he had that the thing to which he had dedicated himself and for which he was prepared to pay the supreme sacrifice would one day capture and sway the hearts of men all over the world.

"I am sent" was no dim recollection of a word spoken on some far-off shore before his earthly life began. It was born out of a deep experience on earth, amid the ways of men and as he heard the cry of the lost. In the cry of the lost he heard the cry of God summoning him to share the agony of his bereaved heart over the yearning emptiness of men.

The poignant words spoken to the Sidonian woman seem at first sight to be disappointing. But when one plumbs their depths one hears the words of a man who had been listening to the cry of wandering sheep far beyond the hills of the land he had just left for a brief respite. The words of the disciples, "She crieth after us," was but the echo of the sigh in his own soul over the wandering human race God had made for fellowship with himself. If we could see this incident in its proper light, a host of inconsequential controversies would cease to disturb us, as we would set about to revive a religion to meet the needs of people. When he said, "I am not sent but unto the lost sheep of the house of Israel," he

was throwing the arguments of his contemporaries back
into their teeth. If your position is right, if religion is as
narrow and confined as your leaders make it out to be,
then this woman should be left in her distress. It is one
thing for a rabbi to work out a doctrine about the ex-
clusiveness of God, to talk about how many times one
should pray, how one should observe the practices of
religion. But it is quite another thing to apply this
religion to life, to life with its pathos and agony.

It is rather strange that much of the time since the
sweet-toned voice of Love sounded over the hills of
Palestine should have been spent in setting up systems of
faith, church organizations which differ from one another, and creeds which deal in metaphysical speculation. Surrounding are human needs, problems which
concern the lives of individuals and of nations; we have
made the tragic mistake of imagining that we could
meet the need by converting our beliefs into definitions.

The essence of the "glad tidings of the Kingdom of
God" which he came to declare can be summed up in
a few words: the substitution of self-forgetting service
for selfish brute force. Consciousness of our indebted-
ness to the infinite love of God toward us in our own
sins and follies issues out in obedience to his will, and
makes us know that his love extends to the greatest and
the least, and that the ultimate principle of morality
which we hope will characterize the life of individuals

and nations everywhere can be accomplished only by self-sacrifice. The kings and rulers of the world exercise lordship, but in the Kingdom of God it is the humble and self-effacing who will bring about the will of God on the earth. His sovereign will is not that of creating men, then damning them for his own glory, but that of an unresting Servant of mankind. He reigns by loving, and he realizes himself through self-effacement, doing the work of a servant, sweeping the earth's floor as the seasons roll round, washing it with his rain, warming its surface with the sun, and lighting it with the lamp of the moon and the stars when night falls. The story of the ages,

> A fire-mist and a planet,
>   A crystal and a cell,
> A jelly-fish and a saurian,
>   And caves where cave-men dwell;
> Then a sense of law and beauty
>   And a face turned from the clod,—
> Some call it Evolution,
>   And others call it God,[22]

is the story of the long patience of God in the creation of the universe.

No less patient has he been with men. He has never grown tired in his efforts to lift mankind to the heights of communion with himself. And when the Light of

Life began to shine into the dark places of men's hearts, God saw in him the one in whose soul he delighted: "I have put my spirit upon him: he shall bring forth judgment to the Gentiles. He shall not cry, nor lift up, nor cause his voice to be heard in the streets. A bruised reed shall he not break, and the smoking flax shall he not quench: he shall bring forth judgment unto truth." [23] When one begins to evaluate the reason for the least advancement in man's long climb to God, one finds it in the lives of those who have spent themselves in the service of men, and found the going hard because of the multitudinous sorrows, oppressions, miseries and wrongs in the world. Jesus found the spirit of the world, not only in the wilderness temptation, but in the Upper Room in Jerusalem on the night before the Crucifixion: "Which of them should be accounted the greatest?" Two thousand years have passed since that night, and the Church has yet to learn that the most majestic, the most awe-inspiring vision of God is his tireless redeeming humility. "Behold, I am among you as he that serveth."

> The time will come when this, one Holy Church
> Shall melt away in ever widening walls,
> And be for all mankind. And in its place
> Shall rise another church, whose covenant word
> Shall be the act of love. Not *Credo* then
> But *Amo* shall be the watchword through its gate.[24]

I have heard much talk on the part of preachers and church leaders about "the revelation of God in Jesus Christ." But Jesus as a "revealer," a mere "enunciator" of the ideas of the Kingdom of God, never seemed quite adequate to express what Jesus set out to be. What he wanted to be, and what he became, was the realization of God in the life of man by humbling himself and by becoming obedient even to the point of uttermost service and sacrifice. He so loved his fellow men that his whole life was dedicated without the least alloy of self to the belief and service of all those who stood in need of them. He came to found a Kingdom, not merely by announcing the laws of the Kingdom, but by letting loose the full tide of divine resources which can be the possession of the living souls of men. It was no mere miracle-working Jesus who saved the life of the woman with the blood hemorrhage. It was the spiritual resources within, and which she exercised at the command of Jesus. "Be of good comfort; thy faith hath made thee whole." His was the task, not of writing the laws of God on the hearts and minds of men, but of releasing the God-given qualities with which men were endowed "when the morning stars sang together, and all the sons of God shouted for joy." [25]

"I and my Father are one" has no reference to his passing from the unseen into time. He was already one with his Father in thought, in feeling, and in moral purpose. Always with the words on his lips, "My Father is greater than I," he stood in childlike humility looking up into the face of God. For what else is humility but

> . . . . that low sweet root
> From which all heavenly virtues
> shoot,[26]

and where but in the lowliness of Jesus do we find the majesty of God?

"I thank thee, Father, Lord of heaven and earth, that thou hast hidden these things from the wise and understanding and revealed them to babes," [27] must have been the burden of his prayers from the hour of that ecstatic experience at the Jordan. When the end was drawing near, one sees the joyous expression on his face as Jesus hears the exciting tales from those whom he had sent into the villages to teach and to preach: "I saw Satan fall like lightning from heaven." [28] Something of the divinity which was his must have caught fire in the souls of the simple friends whom he had called to be with him. To them—fishermen and taxgatherers—and to himself of whom the learned of his day asked, "How knoweth this man letters, having never learned?" [29] God had confided his innermost secrets. Somewhere the call which he heard in the carpenter shop in Nazareth became identified with the secret center of his personality, and the invitation with which a burdened, sorrowing humanity has become so familiar has in it all the yearning heart of God: "Come unto me, all ye that labour and are heavy laden, and I will give you rest. Take my yoke upon you, and learn of me; for I am meek and lowly in heart: and ye shall find rest unto your souls. For my yoke is easy, and my burden is light." [30]

V

Down Among Life's Broken Earthenware

━━━━━━━━━━━━━━━━━━━━━━━━━━━━━━━━━━━━━━━

*H*OLMAN HUNT'S well-known picture, "The Shadow of Death," tells the story of how the world's suffering fell upon the sensitive spirit of Jesus. Standing before the picture one looks into the carpenter shop and sees Jesus facing the open doorway. He has just stood erect and stretched his arms in a gesture of weariness after sawing wood upon a trestle. As he looks out into the waning sunlight his shadow is cast against the rack of carpenter tools on the wall behind him. Shadow and tools together make the rude outline of a figure on a Cross. Jesus does not see it, but his mother sees it as she kneels by the oil jar. Yet the thing in the picture that haunts our souls is the sorrow written on his face.

A kind of sorrow is written on dry-eyed, wrinkled faces which betrays disillusionment and world weariness. There is the sadness of eyes that have looked through life and found that it holds no hope, no ultimate meaning, and no God. Multitudes sit alone with their despair like lonely figures by the shore of a somber and hopeless ocean.

> This life's a hollow bubble,
> Don't you know?
> Just a painted piece of trouble
> Don't you know?
> We come to earth to cwy,
> We grow oldeh and we sigh,
> Oldeh still and then we die.
> Don't you know?[1]

There is sorrow, too, on the countenances of those who are marked for early death. Little children with leukemia may not know all that it means to die so young, and the middle-aged man whose heart has failed draws a sickly smile across the face and lives in the hope that a miracle will yet be worked. But the pathos of it all is reflected in the face of the onlooker. The sight awakens pity, and those of us who see ask ourselves why it is that some inscrutable power has cast its dark shadow on the life.

But the weariness and pain which the artist has painted into the face of the Carpenter of Nazareth was born, not out of hopelessness and despair, nor even out of a sudden premonition of impending death. The Cross was seen at this time only by Mary, and by the time the fancy of the artist painted it on canvas, it was an old, old story. The sorrow-laden face which we see in the picture is the face of a Man who carried a burden on his heart. Acquainted as he was with the prophets, his thoughts must even then have turned instinctively to the mournful story of Hosea, and later made him give it expression as he faced the meticulosities of the Pharisees: "Go ye and learn what that meaneth, I will have mercy, and not sacrifice: for I am not come to call the righteous, but sinners to repentance."[2]

Has any one of us stood before the thorn-crowned Jesus, wearing a purple robe, and with a reed in his hand, without noticing the horror, the pity, the pain, the agony, in the face of the Man who saw the abysses to which the human heart could descend? Whether or not he saw a literal wooden Cross one day in the carpenter shop, long before he stepped for the last time across the threshold of his home he must have seen the moral darkness of his day which was to dog his footsteps until the hour when he cried, "It is finished."

Every great spiritual genius has seen the difference between right and wrong, and that both have eternal significance. Dante saw it when he wrote:

> Good, inasmuch as we perceive the good,
> Kindles our love; and in degree the more,
> As it comprises more of goodness in it.
> The Essence then, where such advantage is,

That each good, found without it, must needs attract
The soul of each one, loving, who the truth
Discerns, on which this proof is built.[3]

Socrates saw it when he said to Simmias: "If the soul is really immortal, what care should be taken of her, not only in respect of the portion of time which is called life, but of eternity! And the danger of neglecting her from this point of view does indeed appear to be awful." [4] Buddha asked: "What kind of individual is he whose deed of wickedness brings him to hell? Whenever an individual is not proficient in the management of his body, in the precepts, in concentration, in wisdom, and is limited and bounded, and abides in what is finite and evil: such an individual is he whose deeds of wickedness bring him to hell." [5] It is thinkers, too, such as Paul, who talked of how men can become "alienated from the life of God," "without God in the world," and "enemies of God." [6] Carlyle, in our modern day, when asked, "Who will be judge?" answered "Hellfire will be judge." And one day when he led Emerson through the worst streets in London at midnight, he asked, "Do you believe in the devil now?"

These seers did not invent sin as a foundation upon which to base religion; they found it in human life. And who does not find it in his own life when he begins to think about himself seriously, if God grows real, and when he gives himself, not to some vague contemplation of God, but to honest study of God's ways in human affairs? "When God matters to a man, all life shows the result. Good and bad, right and wrong, stand out clear as the contrast between light and darkness—they cannot be mistaken, and they matter—and matter forever." [7] The old adage, Sow a thought and you reap an action; sow an action and you reap a habit; sow a habit and you reap a character; sow a character and you reap a destiny, is as true now as it was yesterday. Right and wrong are of eternal significance, and just as physical laws are deducible from the reactions of matter and force, so moral laws have been the genuine discovery of what was clearly existent and operative.

If Jesus had failed to see these fundamental laws of life, it is hardly likely that his teachings would have remained. But he could not have ignored the problem of sin and forgiveness, even had he wished to ignore it. When he preached, "In your patience possess ye your souls," [8] he was talking of life as a probation period where men could grow in character, stand trial and difficulty, and through sacrifice to higher ends find their other selves. He knew the other side, also. Men could unmake themselves. They could surrender themselves to the dominion of evil in such manner as to spoil the pure image of God in the soul.

God is not omnipotent to the point of where he can

grow grapes on a wayside thorn bush, or make thistles bear figs. He cannot stop rust from corrupting, and moths from making good garments worthless. If a man's restless craving for sensuous and lawless excitement should eventually lead him to the place where he becomes lost in a dreary desert of dissatisfaction and utter despair, there is nothing God can do about keeping the soul from becoming a prey to the life-destroying vultures of wickedness. If men insist upon becoming crawling serpents and vipers, loathed and despised by their fellows, there is nothing God can do about that. One can put out of one's mind every conception of a materialistic hell—as one ought to do—built up over the centuries by a penal theology, but one cannot get rid of the picture drawn by Jesus of the rubbage heap one can cast one's soul upon. When he saw it, his pure soul shuddered. When he saw the valley of Gehenna lying beyond a city gate, he saw a place of evil smells where men burned ashes, straw and offal. In this place wandered the homeless pariah dogs, whose gnashing teeth could be heard in the silence of the night. It was a place to which no one wanted to go. Milton describes it as

> The pleasant valley of Hinnom, Tophet thence
> And black Gehenna call'd, the type of hell.[9]

In Jesus' mind it was the dumping ground of the universe where men had lost capacity of will to act, and hardly the conscience to discern because evil had become their good.

We are not required to interpret Jesus' saying, "It must needs be that offences come; but woe to that man by whom the offence cometh," [10] beyond the range of earthly life. To those of us who believe in a sorrowing God, that he sees men, women and little children victimized by fate, knows to what depth of degradation and beastliness man may fall through no inherent fault of his own, and recognizes the twisted personalities which have been hung on countless numbers of people long before they got a fair start in life, we shall have to stand with Whittier who wrote:

> Who fathoms the Eternal Thought?
>   Who talks of scheme and plan?
> The Lord is God! He needeth not
>   The poor device of man.
>
> I walk with bare, hushed feet the ground
>   Ye tread with boldness shod;
> I dare not fix with mete and bound
>   The love and power of God.
>
> . . . .
>
> I see the wrong that round me lies,
>   I feel the guilt within;
> I hear, with groan and travail-cries,
>   The world confess its sin.
>
> . . . .

ONE FINE HOUR

No offering of my own I have,
   Nor works my faith to prove;
I can but give the gifts He gave,
   And plead His love for love.

. . . .

I know not where His islands lift
   Their fronded palms in air;
I only know I cannot drift
   Beyond His love and care.

O brothers! if my faith is vain,
   If hopes like these betray,
Pray for me that my feet may gain
   The sure and safer way.[11]

Jesus knew, and beheld with intense sorrow, how things which were neither good nor bad at the start, just empty, could steal in upon the soul, possess it, and leave the man seven times worse than at the beginning, and getting himself into a far country among swine husks. What other can God do than bend over with a broken heart and whisper, "Lost?" It was right here that Jesus felt the same emotion and experienced the same pain as did God. Yet he lived his life in the midst of the human race, sharing its griefs and its woes, standing as a brother to those who stumbled and wandered, and watched many of them spurn his goodness and go their way into the paths of selfishness which ultimately meant their own, and their nation's, ruin. How to bridge the gap between them and God, how to bring a full life into an empty life, how to show them the goodness of God, his forbearance and his love, and how to be to them forgiveness—this was his problem, and this was the purpose for which he walked the lanes and streets of Palestine. It is this which can be called by no other name than expiation, a closing up of the gap, bringing back the estranged, showing them what God is like, and the length to which God is willing to go to put meaning into human life.

But to regard Jesus as a Man of sad countenance, going about suppressing every note of gladness that rose to the lips of people who were greedy to hear him and to search for the unknown, is to do both him and the cause of Christianity a rank injustice. Abraham Lincoln, who carried as much sorrow in his heart as one human being can well hold, could laugh despite its burden, and laugh heartily. His laugh has been described as "boisterous," "ringing," "happy," "joyous," and "the President's life preserver." A newspaper comment was: "When he smiles heartily it is something good to see." [12] It must have been good to see the smile of Jesus, the twinkle in his eye as he frequently employed that ingenuity called wit with which he adorned his aphorisms, and to hear the chuckle he emitted at the frequent discomfiture of his enemies. His listeners must have smiled that day when he dispelled his critics with the happy proverb: "How wilt thou say to thy brother, Let me pull out the mote out of thine eye; and, behold, a beam is in thine own eye? Thou hypocrite, first cast the beam out of thine own eye; and then shalt thou see clearly to cast out the mote out of thy brother's eye." [13] If laughter, humor, gladness and joy have evaporated from our religion, it is not that Jesus lacked them, but because the severity which we have attached to God in his dealings with the human race has scorched every hilarious and joyous impulse like a thin blue flame. "When Lincoln would be telling a rich story and Stanton would enter, the story and the laughter would die." [14] The Church has housed too many Stantons.

To attach this element of joyous enthusiasm to Jesus is not to imply a denial of the deep, soul-searching experience we have noted as well. It is not to effuse with Ernest Renan: "As happens frequently in the case of lofty natures, his tenderness of heart transformed itself into an infinite sweetness, a vague poetry, a universal charm." [15] Jesus was not a mere visionary, a dreamer, too naïve to know the dark secrets of the mind, He was no man of sanguine temperament, a stupid enthusiast, who was clumsily broken on the wheel of the hard, relentless facts of life.

To be sure, he had the heart of a little child, and he told the world that child-heartedness is the main condition for entering the Kingdom of God. Who does not sense the simplicity and the charm of his words and deeds. He never dealt in the abstract and the obscure. He reveled in the concrete and obvious. Robert Louis Stevenson speaks somewhere of the blessedness of the man who sees clearly and can tell in plain language what he sees. Jesus could do that, and any man who lives in the atmosphere of his mind and spirit has little difficulty in understanding his words and deeds. But to impute to him the innocence of a little child is to misjudge him. One cannot discount the influence of a radiant personality, and no one can deny that the personality of Jesus remained with him like a haunting melody. "Even Roman soldiers could feel that he was different from every other man they had ever known. He had all the faculties and passions of our common humanity, and yet no one had ever had them in the combination and in the strength in which they were found in him." [16]

But far greater than his personality was his penetrating insight. There is no contradiction between simplicity and intellect. When men sit humbly and reverently before a great truth the discernment is sharpened. Intellect is like steel; it must strike against something with the same quality as itself before sparks can be generated. Jesus' heart and mind struck the mind and heart of God, and thus his eye could see straight into the human heart. Any number of people were disconcerted

123

by his ability to read their innermost thoughts. Many did not like it and not a few went away, never to return. "From within, out of the heart of men, proceed evil thoughts, adulteries, fornifications, murders, thefts, covetousness, wickedness, deceit, lasciviousness, an evil eye, blasphemy, pride, foolishness: All these things come from within, and defile the man." [17] Thus Jesus exposed the sham religion practiced by the ecclesiastics of his day and foisted upon the people. What a difference there is between the penetration of Jesus into the sordidness of evil, and the commonplace view which many preachers take of the vices which are prevalent in the world today!

> The Reverend Dr. Harcourt, folk agree,
>   Nodding their heads in solid satisfaction,
> Is just the man for this community.
>   Tall, young, urbane, but capable of action,
> He pleases where he serves. He marshals out
>   The younger crowd, lacks trace of clerical unction,
> Cheers the Kiwanis and the Eagle Scout,
>   Is popular at every function.
>
> And in the pulpit eloquently speaks
>   On divers matters with both wit and clarity:
> Art, education, God, the Early Greeks,
>   Psychiatry, Saint Paul, true Christian charity,
> Vestry repairs that shortly must begin—
>   All things but Sin. He seldom mentions Sin. [18]

One cannot think of Jesus as a carpenter without visualizing a strong body. He had hard muscles, calloused hands, and physical resistance to disease. There is no record of his ever having been sick either during the years in Nazareth or during his ministry when he was exposed to the elements and the hardships of long pilgrimages on foot. He was young and doubtless felt the thrill of being alive. One wonders, if, in addition to his interest in growing grain, birds and flowers, roaming the countryside and climbing the hills, he ever took any risks or sought adventure. If any of us could have lived in his village, have seen his sun-tanned face and body, and beheld the ripple of his muscles, we would have admired him as a young man capable of running a long race, taking risks, and seeking adventure, and wished that we too might be so well equipped physically, perhaps envied him.

But there are strong men in our day who shy away from weakness and disease, who cannot understand why it is that others are not so healthy as they. As for putting themselves out in the interest of less fortunate people, they regard it as an intrusion on their pleasure and comfortable circumstances. Jesus might well have lived in the glow and satisfaction of being a Samson, and living his life among the privileged class. Surely he had the qualities that would have lifted him to a place in Herod's court, or as a member of the Sanhedrin, or a noted

Rabbi. But that was not his character. He chose to live down among life's broken earthenware; in that environment his joy would become full. From the downtrodden he would draw his inspiration. When folk of this class saw him standing in their midst, they did not love him for his vigorous body, nor because he rejoiced in the abundance of health and life; they loved him because they saw a Man with a seamless garment that marked him as a gentleman, who was willing to stoop to their brokenness, interest himself in their sick bodies, their penury, their wanderings, their loneliness, their starved souls, and to do it all at the cost of becoming an outcast himself, oppressed and afflicted, and led as a lamb to the slaughter.

Jesus in the service of the broken is common enough in literature. It is found in James Russell Lowell's poems, "The Vision of Sir Launfall" and "The Search." In the latter he tells how he had sought Jesus in nature, in the halls of the rich, and in the houses of worship. Then turning from his vain quests into the streets of the city, he saw the prints of the bleeding feet:

> I followed where they led,
> And in a hovel rude,
> With naught to fence the weather from his head,
> The King I sought for meekly stood;
> A naked, hungry child
> Clung round his gracious knee,

> And a poor hunted slave looked up and smiled
> To bless the smile that set him free;
> New miracles I saw his presence do,—
> No more I knew the hovel bare and poor,
> The gathered chips into a woodpile grew,
> The broken morsel swelled to goodly store.
> I knelt and wept: my Christ no more I seek,
> His throne is with the outcast and the weak.

The service of Jesus is the service of the broken and the spent. His ejaculation, "Now is my soul troubled," [19] was not a single experience. A troubled soul was a daily experience, and on a hundred occasions he could have pleaded, "Father, save me from this hour."

But beneath it all ran a joy that no man could take from him—the joy of following the direction pointed out by his Father, the joy of serving a cause, of self-expenditure, and the delight of finding opportunities for giving to men the best he had. And what a best! At his command was not the power to take a city, to issue orders, or to become a dictator, making men become his slaves, or asking impertinent questions, or suspecting the people's loyalty to himself and his country, or threatening them with the prospect of a prison sentence. The power he possessed was the power to change men's minds, to enshrine himself in the personality, to drive out disease with his sympathy and the healing power of his love. That is why he ate with publicans and sinners, talked with them, and lived himself into their misery and pain. Men's values would be lifted out of the moral haze of sordidness and greed, and made to be centered on what was clean and simple and natural. That is why he defended them against the cold, suspicious and self-centered goodness of their leaders. He could have wasted his time among the proud and self-satisfied, the anti-social and the antiracial, the men of prominence who played the fiddle and called the tune for the dancers, and who were convinced of their wholeness. Too many preachers do so today, and thus make a mockery of the things Jesus began to do and to teach.

His place was down among the broken. That was the reason why the common people heard him gladly, why they welcomed him, and sought his company. He was far above them, and belonged to a world with which they were not familiar. They had never traveled his road, never prayed as he prayed, and never stood on his mount of vision. But it was easy to rise a little higher and become more like the people they ought to be, just because he had an unquenchable faith in human nature.

When I listened to a lately returned missionary from China say, "You can't trust the Chinese, they will knife you in the back at the first opportunity," I wondered about his missionary enterprise. Paul was "knifed in the back" on many occasions, and the attitude of this missionary is a far cry from the manner in which Jesus walked among the populace of Palestine. He knew the degrading bondage of the passions to which they had sold themselves, and as they looked into his face they knew that he knew. He knew the filth of their bodies, the prejudices, hates and revenges of their minds. Strange, is it not, that he still believed? Matthew, Mary Magdalene, Zacchaeus and the Woman of Samaria are only examples of what must have happened in the hearts of countless others like them. But what had died in them came back to life in his presence. Mourning was turned into dancing, and their sackcloth put off for the garment of gladness. They shed tears, too. But their tears were tears of joy because at last they had caught a glimpse of the pity and pain of the heart that understood and was bearing their shame. Love is always like that, a thing of joy, and a hard thing. It breaks the heart. It heals, but first it wounds.

What about the Master's hope as he prayed, "Thy kingdom come, thy will be done on earth as it is in heaven"? The coming of the Kingdom was his theme song. A letter came to me from a prominent theologian which read: "The Kingdom of God is not for this world. It can't work in politics or in international relations. It can work only in a perfectionist world." Was Jesus mistaken? Was his confidence in its realization born only out of a boyish optimism? We look back two thousand years to the night Judas planted the kiss on his cheek because he thought the ship in which he had been voyaging was about to sink, despaired that it would ever be brought to port by the Captain who was sailing in another direction than that which would restore the glory of Israel's past; then we gaze upon the world today in which the Upper Room in the city of Jerusalem, the Garden of Gethsemane, and the Cross bear scant significance beyond reading matter. The two views seem identical, and we must say that it is not only Judas who loiters in the dark, but councils, churches, factories, philosophies and so-called Christian nations as well, that implant a betraying kiss. When we observe Pilate washing his hands on that black Friday, then delivering Jesus to be crucified, we feel that even now Barabbas is being released, and Pilate's hands are still in the basin.

This ought not so to be. But so it is. The night is black, and is made no brighter by the manner in which the church sidesteps the issues of the Gospel. The gloom may get thicker before the dawn comes, and the dayspring from on high visits us. Still it is unfair to call Jesus a mistaken enthusiast or optimist. If there was one note of absolute assurance on his lips it was that the task to which he had set his hand would be consummated. But to say that he expected it overnight, or in two thousand years, and that his thinking lay in the direction of a swift-conquering victory, is to read into his life and work something that is not there.

Anyone who scans the heart of Jesus as he faced his temptations may well know that with three quarters of the world's population crying for bread, the solution of the problem is not that of merely supplying bread. The freedom of men can be bought only at the price of moral and spiritual victory on the part of us who see the clear light of his counsels in times that are dark. When he refused to do the spectacular and to call upon God to intervene and thus prove his claim to power, he must have looked down the long centuries and seen himself dashed to pieces against the stones of greed, selfishness, hate and misunderstanding, not once, but a thousand times, before men would take up his Cross and follow him. When he refused to bow before the world's method of achieving a Kingdom, he knew that in the long future before the principles of God's Kingdom should be supreme in human hearts, he would have to travel the way of bitterness, sorrow and sacrifice, not once on a wooden Cross, but countless times, in families, in churches, in business and in the parliaments of men.

He was all too familiar with the manner in which the prophets were scorned to be fooled into believing that what he taught would be quickly followed: "Some of them ye shall kill and crucify; and some of them shall ye scourge in your synagogues, and persecute them from city to city." [20] Time and again he reminded his disciples that men would deliver them up to councils, scourge them, and that a prophet would have no honor in his own house and in his own country. If there be any doubt about his knowing the dark doom that would envelop his followers, that doubt is dispelled in "Can the children of the bridechamber fast while the bridegroom is with them?" There was rapt joy in that question, and his followers must have felt for a moment that they would bask in his presence for long years. But the ghost of the near future stole up beside him as he reclined at the feast, and the faces around him grew solemn as he said, "But the day will come when the bridegroom shall be taken away from them, and then shall they fast in those days." To the disciples at this early juncture of his ministry, this was a strange word. But he knew. The shadow had already fallen; a tragic death would be his. Joyful and sure as he was over the prospect of an everlasting Kingdom, he yet knew that it would not be won by a single sacrifice, his own.

How the dogmatists over the centuries have made the salvation of mankind depend upon one single death upon a Cross is puzzling to anyone who knows that the crimson strands of vicarious sacrifice are woven into the texture of all creation. We see the principle struggling up through tangled and thorny paths in the long travel of the earth, and how the life of the weaker has been sacrificed to the stronger or more cunning. In the higher realm of animal life, especially mankind, we see sacrifice breaking out in one show of splendor after the other. Every time a baby is born a mother is involved in sacrifice and pain, and risks death. The sweat and toil and tears of parents are put into the preservation of the young life in the home. If our knowledge would cover the earth every day of our lives would witness the spectacle of men and women giving their lives to save the lives of their fellows. Wherever love lays itself beside wretchedness and misery, wherever innocence bears the shame and guilt of another, wherever compassion and forgiveness becomes the motivating power of any Godly deed, there men are lifted toward the region of the Cross.

The Christians of the churches resent the intrusion of such a spiritual fact upon their lives. They have gone even further: they have laid the sins of the world and their own sins upon the back of one Man, Jesus. They refuse to allow the intrusion of the Cross into our lives. They have made the Cross respectable, even stylish. A parade is staged into the worship of the sanctuary with flags unfurled; the altar is adorned with a golden cross and silver candlesticks; the breaking of bread and the drinking of the cup is surrounded with pageantry; the deity of Jesus is asserted in psalms and hymns sung to his praise. Jesus is worshiped though he wanted to be followed, and his majesty is declared whose only majesty is to be sought in his humility and patience. It is forgotten that the most important act that occurred in the Upper Room was not the Pascal meal, but the doing of the dirtiest, filthiest, most menial and despised task of washing disciples' feet and proclaiming, "If I then, your Lord and Master, have washed your feet; ye also ought to wash one another's feet."

We do not like to hear too much about this because it sets at naught our puny ideas of majesty and dignity and glory. We do not like it because we are sure that this is not the day to tumble wrong from its throne. Faith is mocked and fails miserably, humility is trodden in the dust, and pity is weakness and sympathy is folly. Christians do not like to hear that Jesus was a poor Man all his days, that he had a provincial background, and that he was the child of a despised race, the Jewish, whom many people in our churches today like no better. Christians are annoyed to be reminded that he broke with the accepted religious code of his day, and was found in the company of outcasts with bad reputation; that he was gentle toward criminals and prostitutes, and harsh with priests. Christians are offended at the information that he was spit upon, made a dunce of, was scourged and made to carry his own Cross and was crucified between thieves, while his friends deserted and his enemies taunted him.

The reason we had a Civil War that made our whole beloved land run in streams of blood was because Lincoln was the first man to come to grips with the issues. All that went before was compromise, subterfuge and innuendo. By the time he came and said, "A house divided against itself cannot stand," it was too late to stem the rising tide of hate, revenge and misunderstanding. If we have had wars since, and are looking into the face of another, it is because the Cross had been a stumbling block to a church that argues the necessity of sin and violence, that restricts the Sermon on the Mount to family life, and that does not hope now to begin to live in the Kingdom of God. The Cross is put back there on Calvary's hill to be used in some mysterious fashion as a passport of safe conduct to the realm of everlasting bliss. Thus the tragedy of the Cross has been reduced to a melodrama. So long as the Cross is postponed to a distant future and to a more advantageous time, it is denied altogether.

The argument runs: There is nothing we can do about it; men and nations are violent, and when we get them subdued, and peoples begin to live at peace with one another, it will be time then to take up the Cross; then it will be safe. In the meantime, we will make Jesus a drumbeater and a winsome fellow who brings quiet assurance to our hearts as we sit in churches that God's in his heaven, all's right with the world, and that politicians and pseudo-statesmen have all the answers. All that is needed is to harmonize the discordant notes in our nature, become perfectly integrated personalities, get God on our side, so that life can be faced complacently and men can live comfortable lives. We will make the Church a going concern and get it nailed down to something that is successful and established with some order of belief and creed and ritual.

Men do not seem to know that evil is never afraid of complacency and decency. It is not concerned with how well a man feeds his family, nor how he does his duty to his friends, nor strives for financial security, nor how many church members are on the rolls. The only thing evil fears is the Cross when it gets itself transmuted into the lives of individuals and becomes a channel through which love and forgiveness flow to peoples upon whom men can normally pile their hates and revenges and blows. This is not my conclusion. It does not come out of my little mind. It lives in the hearts of the saints of all ages and was proclaimed by one of them who asked, "Do you not know that the saints will judge the world? And if the world is to be judged by you, are you incompetent to try trivial cases?" [21] It is written in the world's literature that wherever the Cross is realized, and whoever possesses the spirit of forgiveness, there sharing is seen in the fellowship of the agony of God.

When George Eliot in *Adam Bede* describes the scene where Dinah Morris enters the prison to comfort the wretched girl who had murdered her baby and is awaiting execution, she writes: "She felt the divine presence more and more—nay, as if herself were part of it, and it was the divine pity that was beating in her heart and was willing the rescue of this helpless one. . . . 'See, Lord, I bear her on my arms and carry her before thee. . . . I believe—I believe thy infinite love. What is *my* love or *my* pleading? It is quenched in thine. . . .'" Ah, a law does not forgive! But love may and does. What power is there to bring order to a chaotic world than the Cross borne into the dark places of the earth by Christians?

It is true that sometimes men trust and get cheated by the ones they trust. The world is full of senseless, silly people. There are parents who regard children as nuisances. The world knows that Hitler disposed of six million Jews. Envy, greed, lust and hate build up like a mountain in the place we call our world. Often we grow hot and rebellious, bitter and cynical, and demand an eye for an eye and a tooth for a tooth. Still, there is nothing else to do but stand on the ground where Jesus stood, and to set over against this awful, yawning chasm of evil which seems to be tearing the world apart, the only sure ground of God with his power to heal body and mind, and revolutionize all human life and social activity. Once in human life there was given to a Man the power to renew the heart, forgive and redeem. Men believe that. But they must go further: "As many as received him, to them gave he power to become the sons of God, even to them that believe on his name." People are ciphers as Christians if they are not God's light to humanity.

It is not the purpose of this book to outline in detail at what point and in what manner the divine forgiveness is experienced. We have been tracing the paths which Jesus trod, the way he became what he was, the will and obedience which were his, and how he proclaimed a Kingdom which can be the inheritance of all who choose to become sons of God. As one looks at him as he makes his way step by step toward the Cross, and recognizes that his choice of it, regardless of what our Christology may be, was due to his love of men and women, and his faith in God, these emotions must inevitably stir the depths of our souls. First of all, like the disciples on that white ribbon of road just before he came to Jerusalem, we wonder, and then our wonder turns to fear. We set out with him on a normal, human plane, and follow him into experiences which he never anticipated or expected. When it dawns upon us that the way he is walking leads to a Cross, we become afraid. "A man builds up a world of thought for himself—as all do—a scheme of things; and to a man with a thought-out view of the world, it may come with an enormous shock to realize this incredible idea, this incredible truth, of God in Christ." [22] One becomes afraid, and no one has a right not to be afraid. A man is taken into a brand new world, a world of sacrifice, pain, suffering, and where his previous conception of what constitutes joy and happiness will have to be revised. He is afraid for his family and his career, and he hesitates. Where is he leading, and how far are we prepared to go? Will any of us go even as far as the disciples, though we are afraid? There is only one thing that will take us to the end: our love for the Leader. If we love, we will rejoice to be numbered with the people who are with him. We will be stirred at the sacrificial life of Jesus in the imperial disclosure of God as it is gathered up in the wickedness which men heaped on Jesus; how "through the anguish and the shame of such a death, he shone forth like the sun in splendor, a splendor that time has neither tarnished nor dimmed." [23]

Caroline MacDonald tells of a murderer who lay under the sentence of death in a prison in Japan. A woman gave him a Bible to read. He did not find it particularly interesting, until one day he opened it at the story of the trial of Jesus. Then he exclaimed, "This person they called Jesus was evidently a Man who at any rate tried to lead others into the path of virtue, and it seemed an inhuman thing to crucify him simply because he had different religious opinions from others. Even I, hardened criminal that I was, thought it a shame that his enemies should have treated him in this way. . . .

"I went on, and my attention was next taken by the

words: 'And Jesus said, Father, forgive them, for they know not what they do.' I stopped. I was stabbed to the heart, as if pierced by a five-inch nail. What did the verse reveal to me? Shall I call it the love of the heart of Christ? Shall I call it his compassion? I do not know what to call it. I only know that with an unspeakably grateful heart, I believed. Through this single sentence I was led into the whole of Christianity. . . .

"I have been more than twenty years in prison since I was nineteen years of age, and during that time I have known what it meant to endure suffering, although I have had pleasant times as well. I have passed through all sorts of experiences, and have been urged often to repent of my sins. In spite of this, I did not repent, but on the contrary became more and more hardened. And then, by the power of one word of Christ's, 'Father, forgive them, for they know not what they do,' my unspeakably hardened heart was changed, and I repented of my crimes. Such power is not in man." [24] That is what happens when men expose themselves to the grace and truth of Jesus in his love for men.

One can be naught but thrilled to the depths of one's nature by the experience of Jesus carrying with him from Nazareth to the Cross the spiritual urgency and energy that was daily directed toward the reformation and re-demption of men. He walked in a world of willful blindness and that meant sorrow; in a world of proud self-sufficiency with its daily hate and malice, and that meant collision and clash; in a world where just the opposite of love and forgiveness was enthroned, and that in the end meant death. Even so, he would not turn back. The gifts of healing, cleansing and forgiveness had been bequeathed to him, and he would carry them down into the midst of humanity in utter obedience to the Father's will, and at whatever cost of suffering, pain and loss.

The Church will have to answer the question as to whether it too is willing to carry a Cross into the heart, not only of a man, but of a criminally-minded nation. Is the Good News it bears to the world a big stick, or the Gospel of grace and truth?

VI

One Fine Hour Before the Cross

----

*W*HEN Dr. Richard Roberts delivered the Kent Shaffer Memorial Foundation lectures at Yale University, he attached an epilogue in which he related the story of Rogue Herries as told in one of Hugh Walpole's novels. Rogue Herries was a man with a dream. He felt that somewhere in the world there was a perfect love, and all the years of his life he sought it. "He was a man of great native power, of strong turbulent passions; and there was no dark province of his life which he did not explore in the hope of finding this precious thing which eluded him; and it was not there. A man of seventy, his life in retrospect seemed to him to have been a meaningless anarchy, a bitter waste; and he cursed whatever gods there be for their callous mockery. And then—the great moment arrived. The dream came true. At the end he had his hour of perfect love. All the heats and the lusts, the evil and the pain, the guilt and the sorrows of the years fell away from him; and he stood cleansed and fulfilled in his brief paradise. His final judgment on the tale of the years was this: 'Life has a meaning, at last, life has a meaning. One fine hour is enough!' " [1]

"One fine hour is enough!" It is not enough that we should regard the whole life of Jesus as one prolonged impalement on a Cross. It is not enough to recognize that day by day there was a dark and menacing cloud hanging above his head. Unless one can see the crucifixion lighted up with moral and spiritual significance and taking complete possession of his soul; unless it is seen as the utmost sanity in the midst of a mad world; and unless it proclaims in the face of all outward appearances to the contrary, that life has meaning, it lacks final authority in human life in the matter of judgment and redemption.

Long ago when the Psalms of David were collected in one volume, it was found that one poet penned some lines about the greatness and littleness of man, and praised God that, despite his faults and his failures, God had nevertheless made man "little lower than God, and crownest him with glory and honor." [2] In the early years of the Christian era another writer stated that man had not made good, and was not entitled to such praise. But he did not leave it at that. He added that although we do admit man to be crown of God's creation, we do not see all things under his control. In fact, they are very much out of his control. But, "what we do see is Jesus." [3]

To stand before the Cross one fine hour is enough to convince us of its redemptive power. Calvary is a point of sanity in the midst of a mad world, of reason amidst the discords and follies of time. It redeems the past, floods the future with light, and tells us that life has meaning. In our day, as in the past, there is bankruptcy of human wisdom, the violence of corruption with which man has filled the world, and the devastation of life and property, all because Jesus has been regarded as a man with a heart too big for his head, tremendously in earnest yet pathetically ignorant, and entirely too simple-minded to read the signs of the times or to discern the drift of circumstances. Yet to God who had waited long to find One who would make an offering of perfect obedience to him, the crucifixion was a fine hour, and he saw enough to justify his creation of the human race. And for those who look for "new heavens, and a new earth wherein dwelleth righteousness," [4] they will do well to see Calvary as the one light and hope in a dark world, and the promise of a better tomorrow. One fine hour there will save from cynicism, fear and despair.

It is not necessary to set down in exact chronological order the incidents which led to the final breach between Jesus and the nation. It is enough to know that when he stood in opposition to the cherished conceptions of his time, the Cross was the inevitable result. When he challenged religious practices he was striking at those who robbed the Law of its life and soul and wrapped it in the grave clothes of precedent and tradition.

Not all Pharisees, however, were bad. Nicodemus could not have been the only ecclesiastic who came saying, "How can a man be born again?" One cannot judge a whole system by men such as Annas and Caiaphas; and when it is remembered that Jesus did not come to destroy the Law, but to fulfill it, one can find neither bluster nor provocation in his tone. He had no desire deliberately to offend officialdom. His injunction, "These ye ought to have done," must frequently have been spoken by him. But it was never left to stand alone. "Judgment, mercy, and faith" ought not to be left undone. With his free spirit he could have nothing to do with a religion which bound the souls of men and made them slaves to dead formalism. It was truth that concerned him, and by the very truth that was in him he appealed to those about him to fulfill the Law. Always there was the hope of winning Israel—the priests and the people—by the truth he saw so clearly.

But "truth is unwelcome, however divine," [5] and "truth has tough flavors if we bite it through." [6] When the light of God broke out in Jesus, to the point where he not only declared that a man's conscience can be satisfied by obedience to the living law of God but that a pure heart can receive the indwelling spirit of God sufficient to transmit God's forgiveness to men, it was an "unwelcome" truth, and evoked only sneering disdain in the hearts of the officials. The truth that forgiveness could be obtained in some other manner than that of obedience to the external ceremonial system had a "tough flavor" about it which the guardians of religion could not stand.

They watched him as he lived on familiar terms with publicans and sinners. How can a man be good and pure so long as his associates are harlots and outcasts? Even those who had stood with him at John's baptism, and whom he respected, were beginning to suspect him, and their question, "Why do we and the Pharisees fast oft, but thy disciples fast not?" [7] shook his soul and gave him the awesome premonition of disaster. When he violated the strict law of the Sabbath behind which a powerful hierarchy lay entrenched, and declared that the doing of deeds of mercy was more important than obedience to the strict letter of the law, he was striking at their national interests: if the Sabbath law went the occupation of priest and scribe would also go. What should be done with a man who thus interfered with their business? They took counsel against him, removed his name from the synagogue roll, and excommunicated him. "Jesus withdrew himself with the disciples to the sea: and a great multitude [from Galilee] followed him. . . ." [8] Mark and Matthew do not find Jesus appearing in the synagogue again.

"There's none so blind as they that won't see," and "if the blind lead the blind both shall fall into the ditch." [9] But fortunately up to this time the populace loved him. Their hopes were based on the expectation that he was the promised One at last. They loved his strength, his radiance and his sympathy for them. When he was among them their fears were calmed and their sorrows forgotten. But then suddenly temptation struck again, and what he had seen looming up before him in the wilderness took shape and form once more. If only he would avow himself as their Messiah, stay their hunger, satisfy their material interests as he had done when he fed the multitude, they would make him king. [10]

But he fled—fled to the mountaintop where he could be alone with his tears and with his God. He had rejected their overtures, disappointed their hopes, and in doing so incited popular doubt. He was still the one teacher they delighted to hear; but their hope of a Messiah faded and grew thin. Even his friends began to think him strange, and his mother and brethren were sure that his mind was unbalanced. They hoped he would go back to Nazareth with them and live a quiet life. He had grown too earnest, and his life was being burned out in a frenzy of zeal.

This is a different Jesus from the one about whom we

sing our time-honored Christmas carols. We can cuddle the Babe, grow sentimental about him, and pity the mother who had to give birth to him in a cow stable. But he grew up, and the Church has on its hands a mature Man who makes stern demands, disturbs its smugness, and asks us to rearrange our lives so that we can take up a Cross and follow him. No one thinks ill of a church that is kind to a Baby, honors him with a beautifully lighted crèche on the church lawn, and remains itself in the infant stage of Christianity. It gets itself crucified and rises to maturity of life only when it walks the Golgotha slope with a Man whose alleged madness is the only cure for an insane world.

A little while later the officials brought him another step nearer the Cross. This thing he was doing, healing the demon-haunted minds, was the work of the Prince of demons. One wonders why he did not scorch them with his anger. Are we sure he did not? "All manner of sin and blasphemy shall be forgiven unto men: but the blasphemy against the Holy Spirit shall not be forgiven." [11] They had outraged the purest and most sacred thing that had burned in his heart from the days of his childhood, the poise and peace of soul which had been given him by God and which he was letting fall upon disordered minds. Even God himself could not forgive men whose minds were so evil as to mistake goodness for devilishness. There was nothing he could do with minds and hearts out of which poured the evil streams of hate and suspicion. They wanted a sign just as Satan wanted a sign when he asked Jesus to do the spectacular trick of jumping from the pinnacle of the Temple to show that no harm could come to him. But he had no sign to show them except the sign of the prophet Jonah, the sign of truth which shines in the hearts of men when they understand the meaning of God.

The matter of hand-washing sounds today a trivial matter. One wonders why there should have been such anger aroused against Jesus when he called it into question. But the fact behind it was the belief that when one washed one's hands, one washed one's conscience and turned a curse into a blessing. When Jesus told them that the way to God was not by their outward washings, their rules and conventions, but by purity of heart and reverent chastity, he was striking at the strength and security of the whole system of externalism. The officials were quick to seize the opportunity of planting some doubt in the minds of the people against the Man who was casting aspersions upon this fundamental dogma. It began to grow clear to Jesus that his work in establishing the Kingdom of God was being crushed on the one hand by priestly bigotry and prejudice, and on the other hand by the offending superstitious belief of the people.

He knew that so long as he persisted in the way he

had chosen, to the idea of winning the people to a Kingdom where "neither moth nor rust doth corrupt, and
where thieves do not break through nor steal," there
would come a time when in addition to the priestly hate
and the popular offense the Roman world power by
which they were held in slavery would be invoked as the
final means of destroying him. He had seen this world
power back there in the wilderness, and had been told
how he could become the master of it. He had turned
aside from it.

But he did want to win the world. Why not, and why
not in his own way? There were other races in the world
besides his own. If his own were too obtuse, if he had
found himself in a position where no pleading, no God-
filled soul could soften the hard hearts of his own kind,
surely he would find the desired response in Gentile
hearts. Had he not found more faith in a Roman cen-
turion than in all Israel? Had not the people of Nineveh
repented at the preaching of Jonah? Had a pagan queen
not loved the wisdom of the great King Solomon? Was
he himself not greater than Jonah or Solomon? Was
there no precedent to give sanction to the thought that
people in other regions of the world needed and would
accept the ministrations of one of Israel's prophets? "I
tell you of a truth, many widows were in Israel in the
days of Elijah, when the heaven was shut up three years
and six months, when great famine was throughout all

the land; but unto none of them was Elijah sent, save unto Sarepta, a city of Sidon, unto a woman that was a widow. And many lepers were in Israel in the days of Elisha the prophet; and none of them was cleansed, saving Naaman the Syrian." [12] A prophet may have no honor in his own home and among his own people, but among aliens he finds a welcome.

What woe, what anguish, what tears! What disappointment is revealed in the words of judgment he pronounced upon the cities which were dear to him and where words such as he spoke had never been spoken in their streets before! "Alas, Chorazin, and Bethsaiada, too! If Tyre and Sidon had seen the deeds you have seen, they would have wept and repented. And Capernahum, you think well of yourself! You cast me out and made a hell for yourself! Even Sodom and Gomorrah would not have turned away from the feet that have trod your streets. They shall be your judges!" [13]

So with a heart torn with anguish, and struggling with the futility of expending his love upon a people with deaf ears and hard hearts, he set out across the borders of his native land for a period of rest, for a place where he could catch his breath, get his feet planted once again on the ground of faith and trust, and where he could hear the answer to the questions of his own troubled spirit. Once before in these pages we saw him as he looked with pity and compassion upon the

Sidonian woman as she raised her cry in behalf of her epileptic daughter. We shall have to look again upon that scene, not because of another interpretation of the words he addressed to her, but because one wonders why he did not remain out of the clutches of the authorities in Jerusalem.

Had not the call to go to the Gentile world sounded clear and strong? Was not his mind set on a world-wide community of God? It was quiet there and peaceful beneath the mighty Lebanons and within sound of the sea. And when out of the silence of his meditation he heard the pitiful cry of the woman, "O Lord, thou son of David, my daughter is grievously vexed with a devil," it sounded as though he would have to remain and minister to the lonely exiles outside the bounds of Israel's law. Was this not the faith for which he was questing? Where else could he plant the seed of the Kingdom except in the soil of faith and trust? Did not the religious traditions of his own people look puny alongside the pleading of the woman who was willing to accept even the least of God's grace if only the light of hope could once more shine in her heart? Yes, he would grant her request because such faith could not be denied. "O woman, great is thy faith: be it unto thee even as thou wilt." [14]

Strange, indeed, that a man should turn from a situation that promised victory for the cause that lay nearest his heart ever since his carpenter days in Nazareth! With a world of men and women such as this Sidonian waiting for his healing touch upon their minds and spirits, why would he turn and set himself in the direction of his nation's capital? There the wolves of lust and greed, hate and revenge, lurked and waited to destroy him. How would he break through this violent anti-Roman policy that was leading the nation down to ruin, and driving the people deeper and deeper into disbelief in God? He could preach and teach and heal in Sidon. In Jerusalem he would find only a Cross.

Why did Paul, a generation later, say, "Behold, I go bound in the spirit unto Jerusalem, not knowing the things that shall befall me there: Save that the Holy Spirit witnesseth in every city, saying that bonds and affliction abide me?" [15] Politicians in government and ritualists in religion measure the effect of their words and deeds upon themselves and their careers; but not so the prophets. Saints are careless of bonds and imprisonment, and they count not their lives dear unto themselves. They care only for the inner voice which sounds above the call to caution and safety.

Does this mean that he was in the grip of a power that used him as an unwilling servant? Was an omnipotent God urging him on blindfolded and stumbling in the dark, and saying to him, "Never mind, I'll tell you the next step to take, and it will be the right step in spite of your ignorance"? Was it another will playing upon a Man who had no moral intuition of his own? Phillips Brooks answered these questions when he declared that the higher message of God says, "You are a part of God! You have no place or meaning in this world but in relationship to him. The full relationship can only be realized by obedience. Be obedient to him, and you shall shine by his light, not your own. Then you cannot be dark, for he shall kindle you. *Then you shall be incapable of burning with false passion as you shall be quick to answer with the true. Then the devil may hold his torch to you as he held it to the heart of Jesus in the desert, and your heart shall be as inflammable as his.* But as soon as God touches you, you shall burn with a light so truly your own that you shall reverence your own mysterious life, and yet so truly his that pride shall be impossible." [16]

One could go on and on in an attempt to define the will of God, and in the end come no nearer the answer than this of Phillips Brooks. At all events, in the case of Jesus he had laid his mind and heart so close to the mind and heart of God that what he willed God willed, and what he said and did was born in the heart and mind of God from the beginning. When he considered his own task and measured it alongside the secret purpose of God, he found it to be none other than the establishing of the Kingdom of God on earth. This was his cause, and to that he dedicated his loyalty. But before he could do it, he himself had to live the life and obey the principles of the Kingdom in his own being. More than that, he had to do it, not in the Gentile community of Sidon where the possibility of sacrifice and death was remote, but in the environment which would inevitably react adversely. If he could not face death in a cause that was supreme, then the cause would be something less than supreme, and it could never become the ultimately redeeming power of the world. If a cause ought to triumph, and if it is destined by God to triumph, then it must be maintained in the midst of an environment that was bent upon crushing it to death. It must lose itself to find itself, otherwise it ceases to be itself.

Thus he would go back to "the lost sheep of the House of Israel." He would breathe love into the face of the hate which would blot him out on a Cross. He would set a love as great as the love of God against a diabolism so vicious that it would work his own doom. There was no help for it. He could do no other. Love demanded nothing less. Either he would secure his own people's co-operation in building the Kingdom, or they would become the instruments whereby the Cross of sacrifice should shine more and more brightly unto the perfect day.

And the Cross has shone down through the ages as a bright and burning star before men's wondering eyes.

It looked like defeat on the day it was set up on a lonely hill outside a city wall, but almost overnight the law of utmost sacrifice became a dynamic fact, a spiritual power in the midst of human history, and the prized possession of mankind. There was death in the choice of Jesus, but without it the Church would have no reason for existence.

But before that cruel day arrived he realized that the time had come when he should take the disciples into his confidence and unveil to them this day of doom. He began to say unto them, "The Son of Man must suffer many things . . . and be put to death." [17] "Must" is one of the easiest verbs in the English language to conjugate. It is gloriously defective, with its one mood and one tense. But if ever a word weighed a ton it is this same little defective verb. We meet it at all ages and on all levels of life, and it holds us like a tested line of trench. [18] Jesus' use of the word sets before us two alternatives: Either the relentless coil of giant circumstances was dragging him to his Cross like a helpless puppet, in which case we see only a cruel determinism which sets the path men must walk whether they will or no and by no stretch of the imagination be given the name of "God"; or else it is the "must" which carries a person straight into the jaws of hazard and danger in order to achieve a supreme purpose to which the soul is dedicated.

So nigh is grandeur to our dust,
    So near is God to man,
When Duty whispers low, *Thou must*,
    The youth replies, *I can*.[19]

It was this latter compulsion that produced in Jesus the unwavering loyalty of a will utterly surrendered to the God-given vocation of winning the world through sacrifice.

Thus, one day just a little while before he moves toward the city where his lifework shall be consummated, he takes three of his disciples to the Mount of Transfiguration. As we watch him there on the heights of Hermon, and beneath the far-gleaming snows of the summit, we try in vain to catch the full meaning of it all: he is standing on the margin of eternity where time ceases and space vanishes. All that most of us can do is to be reverent watchers of what goes on, for we are only broken lights of him whose eager heart made him doubly conscious of the voice which crowned his earlier experience: "My beloved Son."

In his flesh he stands on Mt. Hermon. But in his spirit he is standing on Mt. Horeb beside Elijah, the rugged prophet of another day who found God, not in the fire and earthquake, but in the still small voice of calm. Elijah is as fiery as in the days of Ahab and Jezebel, and not one whit less violent in his denunciation of the wickedness of his time. But as Jesus moves beside him in spirit, he hears a voice that is meek and tender: "I, too, was tempted to flee from my task. I was jealous for the Lord God of Israel because the people had forsaken his covenant, thrown down his altars, slain the prophets, until I was the only one left, and they sought also to take away my life. I thought I was the only good man left in Israel until God opened my eyes and I saw that there were seven thousand in the land who had not bowed the knee to Baal." [20]

Then the voice trails off, the figure of Elijah recedes, he is alone, and the darkness comes again. But not for long: the light breaks and he sees an old man coming down out of the mountain who wist not that his face shone. It is none other than the great lawgiver and champion of the people's rights, Moses. He walks beside him until he comes to the people down on the plain, and watches him smash the golden image which had been set up in his absence, and hears him say: "This people have sinned a great sin, and have made them gods of gold. Yet now, if thou wilt forgive their sin—; and if not, blot me, I pray thee, out of thy book which thou hast written." [25]

If one listens one may hear Jesus say to Elijah: "Like you, my lifework cannot be in vain. I, too, have followers. Some are a bit ashamed now, but tomorrow they will be a militant, unafraid, adventurous group. And the group will grow, and many will follow my teachings, and the gates of hell shall not prevail against them. My death will not be a death, but a marching into the land of promise." And in the presence of Moses he would pray: "If thy presence go not with me, carry us not up hence." [22] If thou art with me, I will fear no evil; death will not be death. Art thou with me? Am I truly thy called and chosen servant? Am I the prophet raised to speak the last, best word to men? I, too, am ready to be blotted out for my people. Even so, Father, for thus it seems good in thy sight, if, by my sacrifice, thy reconciling love can stand forth radiant and compelling before the lost sheep. Like sheep they have gone astray. Lay on me the iniquity of them all. I'll be thy suffering servant. Just so there is victory beyond and I shall see of the travail of my soul when I have been the lamb led to the slaughter, and have given my life a ransom for many.

Comforted and strengthened by these holy memories, he becomes one with the deep instincts and longing of his Father. His heart is turned in compassion toward the world until down through the silence around him he hears once more the voice of God's delight in him: "This is my beloved Son: hear ye him."

The sleeping disciples awake. They see no man save Jesus only, kneeling, and on his face the majestic impress of a deep resolve. "It was no fabricated fables that we followed when we reported to you the power and advent of our Lord Jesus Christ; we were admitted to the spectacle of his sovereignty, when he was invested with honour and glory by God the Father, and when the following voice was borne to him from the sublime Glory, 'This is my son, the Beloved, in whom I delight.' " [23]

He had made his last decision there on the Mount. Henceforth, all his movements took him straight toward Annas and Caiaphas and the judgment hall of Pilate.

It was no easy matter to convince the disciples of the coming doom. At Caesarea Philippi, on the eve of his departure for Jerusalem, and on their way going up, he told them, "The Son of man must suffer many things, and be rejected of the elders, and of the chief priests, and scribes, and be killed." [24] Such sacrifice was not within their purview. Indeed, one wonders why he did not discourse at length upon his coming death, and make it as plain as a pikestaff. The only answer one can make to such inquiry is that no man talks much about his deepest agony and brokenheartedness. What he utters on such a theme are not free-flowing discourses, but only groans. These experiences are too deep for words.

It must have been so with Jesus as he thought of what was awaiting him in Jerusalem. Yet, he would let them know that in the light of what would be achieved by his dying, the world around him appeared sunk in an idle dream. He would give them a truth which the world after two thousand years has not yet plumbed: "He that saveth his life shall lose it, and he that loseth his life for my sake shall find it. What shall it profit a man if he gain the whole world and lose his own soul?" [25] The Cross is ours if we choose to take it up, but beyond the Cross lies life eternal. What does a little time here mean if, at its end, the soul is despoiled, life forfeited and lost?

To one light-hearted soul among the few who still followed, he said "Foxes have holes, and birds of the air have nests; but the Son of man hath not where to lay his head." To another who felt he owed filial love to his father, he said, "Let the dead bury their dead." To still another who took the command of Jesus as something which could be fulfilled after all other obligations had been attended to, he replied, "No man, having put his hand to the plough, and looking back, is fit for the kingdom of God." There was no time for dawdling. The path ahead was the path of consecration, with death at the end. "Think not that I came to send peace on earth: I came not to send peace, but a sword," the sword that severs clean the life of spiritual consecration from the familiar ties of the world.

He seemed impatient to go. Once he had a sweet and happy life in Galilee, but that had faded from his interest. There is extraordinary pathos in the words, "Today and tomorrow I must work, and the third day I will complete my task. But I must journey on today, tomorrow, and the next day: it would never do for a prophet to perish except in Jerusalem." [26] He appeared to be chafing at the delay.

> To-morrow, and to-morrow, and to-morrow,
> Creeps on this petty pace from day to day
> To the last syllable of recorded time.[27]

Yonder he strode on the road. He had his face set toward Jerusalem. His cheeks were pale, his lips set. He was anxious to drink the cup of heroic obedience. His pace quickened, the disciples fell behind. They stumbled on; watching his face, seeing the gleam in his eye, they exchanged glances, filled with wonder and fear.

"Anyone who will really try to grapple with this problem of the Cross will find very soon the same thing. . . . If our criticism of Jesus is to be sound, we shall have to learn that we are not as near to him as we imagined. He eludes us, he goes out beyond what we grasp or conceive; and I think the education of the Christian man or woman begins anew when we realize how little we know about Jesus. The discovery of our ignorance is the beginning of knowledge. Plato long ago said that wonder is the mother of philosophy, and he was right. John Donne, the English poet, went further and said, 'All divinity is love or wonder.' When a man begins to wonder about Jesus Christ in earnest, Jesus comes to be for him a new figure." [28] When he chose the disciples he chose them because he wanted them to be with him. To understand him we, too, must be with him. We have to know him before we can understand him.

But the life story of Jesus does not end on the Cross. "There they crucified him" are not the last words in the Gospel. They are not the answer to the man who believes that life has meaning, significance and purpose. To attempt a detailed argument in support of the resurrection of Jesus or the immortality of the soul is not within the intention of this book. We shall have to rest our faith in the words of Jesus: "Destroy this temple, and in three days I will raise it up," [29] and in "God, the soul, and conscience, as integral phrases of reality. If we are materialistic, or mechanistic in our thought, then there is no reason why we should believe in immortality, and many reasons why we should not. If honest as Thomas H. Hardy, we will say, even by the grave of our beloved, as he by the grave of his dear son, 'I neither deny or affirm the immortality of man.' We stand neutral! But if we accept the spiritual interpretation of life, then we must likewise accept the conception of man's survival after death. To reject it, or even doubt it, would be to cut one link of the chain which binds the whole together. It would be to falter in following through the rigorous logic of our own thought." [30]

Let those who will explain the how of the resurrection. I have never tried to explain it. In the end all explanations fail. But take away the resurrection, however, it happened, and the whole history of Christianity collapses. We dwell in a rational world, a world in which divers truths which we know are true remain unexplained. Great results have great causes, and we are sure that somewhere between the crucifixion and the first preaching of the disciples something happened that entirely changed that group of frightened men. Not only did it change them, but it changed the whole history of the world. The evidence for the resurrection is not so much that we read the account of it in the Gospels, as what we find transpired in the disciples—a new life. At sight of the Cross they ran away. A few weeks later they are found rejoicing to be beaten, imprisoned and put to death. Some of their performances—their quarreling, their divisions, and the strange theologies which the early Church wove about the person of Jesus— may all seem irrelevant to the manner in which Jesus set about to be the doer and achiever of something far greater than the mind of the theologian conceived. Nevertheless, if the Gospel stops with the crucifixion, then God remains unexplained, and the story ends in tragedy.

We are not bound to give the resurrection reports a literalistic interpretation, but we are constrained to believe that the whole world of men is altered when we believe that the death of Jesus was not doom to him and to mankind but victory. "At that very hour some Pharisees came, and said to him, 'Get away from here, for Herod wants to kill you.' And he said unto them, 'Go tell that fox, "Behold, I cast out demons and perform cures today and tomorrow, and the third day I finish my course." ' " [31] Herod could kill him. What did it matter? He would rise again and live again in the world and in the hearts of all he had ransomed.

In the Upper Room he took the cup and said, "This is my blood of the new testament, which is shed for many." The ripe fruit of the Father's vineyard would be pressed in the wine press of Israel's hate, pride, and scorn, and the holy spirit of God would be distilled in one draught of forgiveness. Jesus held in his hand the silver chalice of a perfect obedience.

But he had another cup to drink, the cup of the agony of Gethsemane. "O my Father, if it be possible, let this cup pass from me." He shuddered and sweat blood-drops of anguish. He had long since overcome the fear of physical death. He did not fear that victory was slipping from his grasp. But there loomed the black evil that was closing about him, the loneliness, the repudiation by his own people, the fair-weather followers who turned back and walked no more with him, spurious popularity that had given way to suspicion, the pride of the officials that turned to bitter hate, the misunderstanding of disciples who had grown afraid and become estranged.

Mocking and scourging would be visited upon him whose only passion was the need of men and the showing of the face of God to them. The darkness was growing darker. Could he endure it? Could God demand such suffering that he drink the dregs of the bitter cup! Would God let his countenance fall on him? Or, if he refused to drink, would he lose God? What was he to do?

There was only one thing to do: obey! "Not my will, but thine be done." On the Cross God seemed to draw away from him until the cord of his faith almost snapped. We hear the cry: "My God, my God, why hast thou forsaken me?" His mind went back to the Psalmist who uttered the same cry. What did he do? He remembered: "The meek shall eat and be satisfied: they shall praise the Lord that seek him: your heart shall live for ever. All the ends of the world shall remember and turn unto the Lord: and all the kindreds of the nations shall worship before thee. For the kingdom is the Lord's: and he is the governor among the nations." [32] Forsaken? Yes. Still, "My God, my God!" What a fool! But "Where is the wise? where is the scribe? where is the disputer of this world? hath not God made foolish the wisdom of this world? . . . the Jews require a sign, and the Greeks seek after wisdom: but we preach Christ crucified, unto the Jews a stumblingblock, and unto the Greeks foolishness; but unto them which are called, both Jews and Greeks, Christ the power of God, and the wisdom of God." [33]

His body was exhausted, he bowed his head, and before he expired, he uttered the last word of faith, "Father, into thy hands I commend my spirit." He had kept his word: "Thou shalt worship the Lord thy God, and him only shalt thou serve." One fine hour before the Cross is enough to save us from cynicism, despair and unfaith.

> Whenever there is silence around me
> By day or by night—
> I am startled by a cry.
> It came down from the cross—
> The first time I heard it.
> I went out and searched—
> And found a man in the throes of crucifixion,
> And I said, "I will take you down,"
> And I tried to take the nails out of his feet.
> But he said, "Let them be
> For I cannot be taken down
> Until every man, every woman, and every child
> Come together to take me down."
> And I said, "But I cannot hear you cry.
> What can I do?"
> And he said, "Go about the world—
> Tell everyone you meet—
> That there is a man on the cross." [34]

Notes

I. A Venture upon God into the Unknown

1. Fritz Kunkel, *Creation Continues*, p. 49.
2. Isa. 11:9.
3. Matt. 11:25, 26 (a.s.v.).
4. Matt. 11:27; cf. Luke 10:22.
5. Walter E. Bundy, *Our Recovery of Jesus*, p. 312.
6. "A parchment, rectangular in shape and inscribed with the passages Deut. 6:4–9, and 11:13–21, written in twenty-two lines. The parchment was rolled up and inserted in a case or tube, which was affixed in slanting position, to the upper part of the right-hand door-post." —*Hastings Bible Dictionary*.
7. Deut. 6:4.
8. Apion 2, 178, 204.
9. Ex. 3:14.
10. Alex. Irvine, *My Lady of the Chimney Corner*.
11. Matt. 18:10; Luke 1:28.
12. Luke 11:5–13; cf. Matt. 7:9–11, Luke 15:11–32.
13. Shirley Jackson Case, *A New Biography of Jesus*, pp. 206 f.
14. *Life of Josephus*.

15. V. G. Simkovitch, *Toward the Understanding of Jesus*, pp. 30, 31.
16. Luke 1:79 (R.S.V.).
17. Matt. 5:43–45.
18. Matt. 11:28–30.
19. Eph. 4:13.
20. Ps. 2:7.
21. Ps. 8:3.
22. Phil. 2:8, cf. Heb. 5:8.

II. How His Soul Stood at Ease before God

1. John 7:46.
2. Mark 2:12.
3. Luke 5:26.
4. J. A. Robertson, *The Spiritual Pilgrimage of Jesus,* pp. 52 f.
5. Harry Emerson Fosdick, *The Manhood of the Master*, p. 147.
6. II Cor. 10:1.
7. Matt. 11:25; Luke 10:21.
8. Matt. 11:27; Luke 10:22.
9. Matt. 11:29.
10. Matt. 5:35.
11. Mark 10:18.
12. Luke 12:5.
13. Matt. 18:14.
14. Matt. 5:8.
15. Adolph Harnack, *What Is Christianity?* p. 21.
16. John Masefield, "The Everlasting Mercy," from *Poems.*

Notes

Copyright, 1911, 1939, by John Masefield. Used by permission of The Macmillan Company.

17. Alfred Noyes, "The Old Skeptic," from *Collected Poems*, Vol. I, by Alfred Noyes. Copyright, 1913, 1941, by Alfred Noyes, published by J. B. Lippincott Company. Used by permission of the publishers (also A. P. Watt & Son and Wm. Blackwood & Sons, Ltd.).
18. Matt. 18:6.
19. Shelley, "Epipsychidion."
20. Matt. 6:28; John 3:8; Matt. 16:2; Matt. 5:45; Luke 9:58; Luke 15:4; Matt. 8:12; Matt. 23:37.
21. Luke 15:7–10.
22. Job 38:7.
23. Luke 9:48 (Moffatt).
24. John 7:17.
25. Luke 2:10.
26. Matt. 7:29.
27. Thoughts, chap. 2, p. 10.
28. Matt. 7:8, 11.
29. Isa. 1:18.
30. Isa. 40:28, 29.
31. Sarah Henderson Hay, "The Shape God Wears."
32. Luke 17:20, 21.
33. J. A. Robertson, *The Spiritual Pilgrimage of Jesus*, p. 81.
34. Phil. 3:7.
35. *Confessions* 9:1.
36. Luke 10:18.
37. Matt. 6:22.
38. Frederick Lewis Allen, *The Big Change*, p. 83.

39. I Tim. 6:17.
40. Matt. 15:3.
41. Isa. 53:4, 5.

III. THE WORLD A DIVINE-HUMAN BROTHERHOOD

1. John Dryden, "The Hind and the Panther."
2. Lord Tweedsmuir (John Buchan), *Pilgrim's Way.*
3. John 6:38; cf. 8:28.
4. Mark 2:16.
5. Matt. 5:17.
6. Luke 4:18, 19.
7. Luke 9:56.
8. Luke 19:10.
9. Mark 10:45.
10. Elizabeth Barrett Browning, "Aurora Leigh."
11. Matthew Arnold, *Memorial Verses*, Stanza 3.
12. Rufus Jones, *Fundamental Ends of Life*, p. 86.
13. William James, *Varieties of Religious Experience*, p. 428.
14. John Oxenham, *The Vision Splendid.* Copyright, 1918, by George H. Doran Co., 1947, by Erica Oxenham. Used by permission of Erica Oxenham.
15. Matt. 8:17; cf. Isa. 53:4.
16. Matt. 9:36.
17. I Kings 22:17.
18. Isa. 35:8, 10.
19. Matt. 23:37.
20. Gen. 1:2 (Moffatt). The marginal reference is "brood."
21. William Vaughn Moody, "The Fire Bringer."
22. Matt. 25:35–40.

23. Angela Morgan, "God Prays." Used by permission of Angela Morgan.
24. Rom. 8:26.
25. John 4:14 (Moffatt).
26. "Jesus, Thou Joy of Loving Hearts," anonymous.

IV. The Urge that Drove Him to His Task

1. Ps. 94:3.
2. Luke 3:5.
3. Luke 9:58.
4. James Black, *The Dilemma of Jesus*, p. 18.
5. Matt. 3:14, 15.
6. Oscar Holtzmann, *Life of Jesus*, p. 137.
7. George Bernard Shaw, *St. Joan*.
8. Ps. 2:7.
9. Isa. 42:1.
10. Oscar Holtzmann, *op. cit.*, p. 137.
11. Emerson, *Immortality*.
12. I Cor. 10:12.
13. Matt. 4:4, 7, 10; cf. 8:3, 6:16, 13.
14. John 4:32, 34.
15. Deut. 8:3.
16. J. A. Robertson, *The Spiritual Pilgrimage of Jesus*, p.166.
17. Mark 1:15.
18. Jer. 20:9; I Cor. 9:16.
19. Matt. 9:37; cf. John 4:35 (Moffatt).
20. Luke 11:49–51 (Moffatt).
21. Luke 12:50 (Moffatt).
22. William Herbert Carruth, "Each in His Own Tongue,"

ONE FINE HOUR

from *Each in His Own Tongue and Other Poems.*
Used by permission of Mrs. William Herbert Carruth.

23. Isa. 42:1–3.
24. Henry B. Carpenter, "Liber Amoris."
25. Job 38:7.
26. Thomas Moore, "Third Angel Story."
27. Matt. 11:25 (R.S.V.).
28. Luke 10:18 (R.S.V.).
29. John 7:15.
30. Matt. 11:28–30.

V. Down among Life's Broken Earthenware

1. Edmund Vance Cooke, *Fin de Siècle.* Used by permission of The McBride Company, Inc. Bacon said this, too.
2. Matt. 9:13; cf. Matt. 12:7, Hos. 6:6.
3. Dante, *The Divine Comedy,* Canto 26.
4. *Phaedo.*
5. Buddha, *Fruitful and Barren Karma.*
6. Eph. 4:18; 2:12; Rom. 5:10.
7. T. R. Glover, *The Jesus of History,* p. 140.
8. Luke 21:19.
9. *Paradise Lost,* 1:404.
10. Matt. 18:7.
11. "The Eternal Goodness."
12. J. G. Randall, *Mid-Stream,* p. 59.
13. Matt. 7:4, 5; cf. Luke 6:41, 42.
14. Randall, *op. cit.,* p. 69.
15. *Life of Jesus,* pp. 25, 26.
16. Charles E. Jefferson, *Character of Jesus,* p. 101.

17. Mark 7:21.
18. Phyllis McGinley.
19. John 12:27.
20. Matt. 23:34.
21. I Cor. 6:2 (R.S.V.).
22. T. R. Glover, *The Jesus of History*, p. 182.
23. Richard Roberts, *That Strange Man on His Cross*, p. 41.
24. *A Gentleman in Prison*, pp. 78, 79, 82.

VI. ONE FINE HOUR BEFORE THE CROSS

1. *That Strange Man on His Cross*, pp. 131, 132.
2. Ps. 8:5 (A.S.V.).
3. Heb. 2:8, 9.
4. II Pet. 3:13.
5. Cowper, "The Flatting Mill."
6. George Eliot, "Armgart."
7. Matt. 9:14.
8. Matt. 12:15; cf. Mark 2:13.
9. Swift, *Polite Conversation*, Dialogue III; Matt. 15:14.
10. John 6:15. Why this incident was left to John's Gospel to relate we do not know. But in each of the Synoptics we learn that after the feeding, Jesus went away to be alone. John's narrative is the only reasonable explanation. He did not want to be king.
11. Matt. 12:24, 31; cf. Luke 11:15.
12. Luke 4:25–27; cf. I Kings 17:10–16, II Kings 5:9–14.
13. Matt. 11:21–23.
14. Matt. 15:22, 28.
15. Acts 20:22 f.

16. *The Candle of the Lord*, p. 17. Italics mine.

17. Mark 8:31; Matt. 16:21; Luke 9:22.

18. Rufus Jones, *The World Within*, pp. 71 f.

19. Emerson, "Voluntaries."

20. I Kings 19:10; cf. Rom. 11:1–4.

21. Ex. 32:31.

22. Ex. 33:15.

23. II Pet. 1:16, 17 (Moffatt).

24. Mark 8:31; cf. Mark 9:31, 10:33–34, Matt. 16:21, 17:22–23, 20:18–19, Luke 9:22, 44, 18:31–33.

25. Matt. 16:25 f.

26. Luke 13:32 f. (Moffatt).

27. Shakespeare, *Macbeth*.

28. T. R. Glover, *The Jesus of History*, p. 167.

29. John 2:19; cf. Mark 15:29.

30. John Haynes Holmes, *The Affirmation of Immortality*, pp. 21, 22.

31. Luke 13:31, 32 (R.S.V.).

32. Ps. 22:26–28.

33. I Cor. 1:20, 22–24.

34. Elizabeth Cheney, "A Man on the Cross."

Set in Intertype Baskerville
Format by Edwin H. Kaplin
Manufactured by The Haddon Craftsmen, Inc.
Published by HARPER & BROTHERS, *New York*